HENRIK IBSEN: PEER GYNT

HENRIK IBSEN

Henrik Ibsen (1828-1906) began his career working in the theatre, and writing romantic history plays influenced by Shakespeare and Schiller. In the 1860s he moved abroad to concentrate on writing. He began with two verse dramas, *Brand* and *Peer Gynt*, and in the 1870-80s wrote the sequence of realistic prose plays for which he is best known, including *Pillars of Society, A Doll's House, The Wild Duck, The Lady from the Sea* and *Hedda Gabler.* His last group of plays, dating from his return to Norway in the early 1890s, are symbolic melodramas: *The Master Builder, Little Eyolf, When We Dead Awaken.* Illness forced him to retire in 1900, and he died six years later after a series of crippling strokes.

KENNETH McLEISH

Kenneth McLeish, born in 1940, has written over 60 books including *The Theatre of Aristophanes, Shakespeare's People A-Z, The Penguin Guide to the Arts in the 20th Century* and *The Bloomsbury Good Reading Guide.* His translations, of plays by all the Greek and Roman dramatists, of Ibsen, Feydeau and Labiche, have been widely performed on radio, TV and the stage. In 1988 Declan Donnellan of Cheek by Jowl directed his version of Sophocles' *Philoctetes.* In 1989 Deborah Warner directed his translation of Sophocles' *Electra* for the RSC, and in 1990 the present version of *Peer Gynt* opened at the Royal National Theatre, London.

in the same series

Stephen Bill, Anne Devlin & David Edgar	*Heartlanders*
Howard Brenton & Tariq Ali	*Iranian Nights*
Howard Brenton	*H.I.D. (Hess is Dead)*
Caryl Churchill	*Cloud Nine* *Icecream* *Light Shining in Buckinghamshire* *Traps*
Martin Crimp	*Dealing with Clair* *Play with Repeats*
Nick Darke	*Kissing the Pope*
Peter Flannery	*Singer*
Alexander Gelman/ Stephen Mulrine	*A Man with Connections*
Henrik Ibsen/Arthur Miller	*An Enemy of the People*
Mike Leigh	*Smelling a Rat & Ecstasy*
Terrence McNally	*Frankie and Johnny in the Clair de Lune*
Arthur Miller	*Playing for Time*
Joshua Sobol/David Lan	*Ghetto*
Michael Wall	*Amongst Barbarians*
Nicholas Wright	*Mrs Klein*

HENRIK IBSEN
PEER GYNT
A Poetic Fantasy

Translated and adapted by
Kenneth McLeish

NICK HERN BOOKS

A division of Walker Books Limited

ROYAL NATIONAL THEATRE

London

Kenneth McLeish's translation and adaptation of Henrik Ibsen's *Peer Gynt* first published as an original paperback in 1990 jointly by the Royal National Theatre, London, and Nick Hern Books, a division of Walker Books Limited, 87 Vauxhall Walk, London SE11 5HJ.

Front cover illustration: detail from *Frühmorgenflug* by Emil Nolde. Reproduced with permission by courtesy of Nolde-Stiftung Seebüll

Printed and set by Expression Printers Ltd, London N7

British Library Cataloguing in Publication Data
Ibsen, Henrik, *1828-1906*
    Peer Gynt.
1. Drama in Norwegian, 1800-1900 – Texts
    I. Title   II. McLeish, Kenneth
    839.8226

ISBN 1-85459-067-7

Introduction

Ibsen wrote *Peer Gynt* in 1867. He intended it as a poetic fantasy, to be read on the page rather than performed on stage. He thus allowed his fancy to lead wherever it wanted: setting scenes in the Sahara desert, giving speaking/singing parts to dewdrops, showing us troll children in their cavern under the mountain, monkeys pelting Peer Gynt with dung in a palm-grove, men in the swirling North Sea after a shipwreck.

Peer Gynt was quickly recognised as a masterpiece of Scandinavian literature, of equivalent status to Goethe's *Faust* in Germany or Manzoni's *I promessi sposi* in Italy. Its roots were in Norwegian folklore – Peer's early adventures are borrowed from Asbjørnsen's *Norwegian Fairy Tales* – and in such 19th-century Romantic novels as those of Sir Walter Scott, where selfless heroines are beacons of redemption in a treacherous, cruel world. Ibsen also filled the piece with satire: of the new 'science' of archaeology, of superstition and above all of the 'back to nature' movements of the 1860s: his trolls believe in making their own clothes and eating such 'organic' foods as cowdung and bullpiss, and one of his lunatics fights for the purity of the ancient language, unsullied by importations from foreign tongues – a preoccupation of mid–19th century Norwegian intellectuals. But Ibsen denied serious purpose in any of this. He meant *Peer Gynt* to be fast-moving, funny and above all fantastical, and if people asked him why he included this or that scene he answered 'Because I felt like it'.

In 1876 Ibsen adapted *Peer Gynt* for stage performance (the production for which Grieg wrote incidental music). His main task was to cut the piece, by about one third. Originally he suggested removing all Peer's African adventures, and replacing them with a symphonic poem on 'world travels' by Grieg, but eventually he chose instead to make hundreds of short cuts, a few lines or speeches in every scene, so that the structure of the piece remained intact. The resulting play was performed, after the manner of the time, with a full orchestra in the pit, and the length of Grieg's incidental movements is explained by the use of naturalistic scenery, and the resulting need for long gaps between scenes, while the sets were changed.

Ibsen hated the idea of *Peer Gynt* being translated into prose. But he meant the piece to be read, not acted, and it seems to me that if *Peer Gynt* is to succeed on stage, in English, a mixture of prose and verse gives more of the original 'flavour' than a wholly verse translation. Ibsen's text is in rhyme, in an assortment of metres. Its language is however simple and colloquial. In Norwegian, this gives the effect of folk-tale. Unfortunately, in English, it can sound like pantomime. Hence my decision to mix prose and verse. I used verse at moments of high fantasy or lyricism – in Ibsen's metres, and rhymed where musical setting seemed indicated. I used prose for ordinary dialogue, and kept Ibsen's blend of colloquialism and luxuriant metaphor. The slang, in particular, has a literary tang similar to Ibsen's.

I have cut the piece according to Ibsen's own suggestions, taking out sentences and phrases rather than whole scenes, and leaving the ebb and flow of the dialogue intact. I think that this is important, as the balances between robustness and sentimentality, philosophy and fantasy, satire and seriousness, are precisely planned and vital to the play. *Peer Gynt* falls into two more or less equal halves: Scenes 1–15, set in Norway during Peer's youth, and Scenes 16–37, showing his travels and his return, in old age, to Norway. In the 1990 Royal National Theatre production, we followed the common custom of casting two actors as Peer, one for each half of the play. 'Younger Peer' is in his early twenties. 'Older Peer' begins in middle age, and ends in his seventies.

The bulk of the cuts are in the African scenes (16–28), which contain a good deal of 1860s political satire, not too comprehensible nowadays, and an enormous amount of repetition. (The original piece was divided into five Acts: scenes 1–3, 4–11, 12–15, 16–27, 28–37.) To ease design problems, I have added a few words to the dialogue here and there to indicate where scenes are happening. The theatre jokes are in the original.

Kenneth McLeish, 1990

PEER GYNT

This adaptation of *Peer Gynt* was first staged in the Olivier auditorium of the National Theatre.

First preview was 9 February 1990; press night was 28 February 1990.

The cast was as follows (in order of speaking):

ÅSE, *a farmer's widow*	Mona Hammond
YOUNGER PEER GYNT, *her son*	David Morrissey
ASLAK, *a blacksmith*	Edward Harbour
STEWARD	Oscar Quitak
MADS MOEN, *the bridegroom*	David Schneider
MADS MOEN'S FATHER	John Matshikiza
YOUNG MAN AT WEDDING	William Hart
SOLVEIG'S FATHER	Jeffrey Segal
SOLVEIG, *a farmer's daughter*	Sara Mair-Thomas
MADS MOEN'S MOTHER	Alison Peebles
SOLVEIG'S MOTHER	Jennifer Hill
INGRID'S FATHER	Philip Voss
INGRID, *the bride*	Sandy McDade
THREE HERDGIRLS	Anna Healy
	Nicola Slade
	Meera Syal
WOMAN IN GREEN	Alison Peebles
OLD MAN OF THE MOUNTAIN	Philip Voss
TROLL CHAMBERLAIN	Charles Simon
HELGA, *Solveig's sister*	Valerie Hunkins
KARI, *Åse's neighbour*	Meera Syal
TROLL CHILD	Jeremy Swift
OLDER PEER GYNT	Stephen Moore
TRUMPETBLAST, *a Swedish businessman*	Jeffrey Segal
COTTON, *an American businessman*	Wyllie Longmore
BALLON, *a French businessman*	Oscar Quitak
EBERKOPF, *a German businessman*	Edward Harbour
MOROCCAN OFFICER	Jonathan Donne
A THIEF	Neil Salvage
ANOTHER THIEF	Jeremy Swift
ANITRA, *a desert maiden*	Meera Syal
STATUE OF MEMNON	William Hart
BEGRIFFENFELD, *keeper of the Cairo madhouse*	John Matshikiza
SCHLINGENBERG, *a warder*	Merlin Shepherd
FUCHS, *another warder*	Jonathan Donne
SCHAFMAN, *another warder*	Neil Salvage

MIKKEL, *another warder* William Hart
EGYPTIAN, *carrying mummy,* Wyllie Longmore
HUSSEIN Sandy McDade
SHIP'S CAPTAIN Wyllie Longmore
SHIP'S COOK Jeremy Swift
STRANGE PASSENGER Philip Voss
PRIEST Oscar Quitak
BUTTON MOULDER Charles Simon
THIN PERSON David Beames

VILLAGERS, WEDDING GUESTS, TROLLS, THE BØYG, SLAVES, DESERT MAIDENS, LUNATICS and THE SHIP'S CREW played by the Company

Directed by Declan Donnellan
Designed by Nick Ormerod
Lighting by Rick Fisher
Music by Paddy Cunneen

All music played live by the Company

Pronunciation Guide

NB Stressed syllables are in capitals. Final 'e' is a short version of the 'e' in 'father' (but without the 'r')

ÅSE   OH-se
APIS   AY-piss ('ay' as in 'hay')
ASLAK   ASS-lak
BROSE   BROH-se
EIVIND   AY-vind ('ay' as in 'hay')
FOLGEFÅNN   FOL-ge-fohn
GJENDIN   GYEN-deen
GRANE   GRAH-ne
HAEGSTAD   HEG-sta
HALLINGSKARVEN   HAL-ings-kawr-ven (short 'a')
HARTEIGEN   HAR-tay-gen ('ay' as in 'hay')
INGRID   EEN-gree
JØKEL   YE(R)-kel ('r' silent)
KARI   KAW-ree
LUNDE   LOON-de
MADS MOEN   Mads MOHN
PEER GYNT   Pear GÜNT (ü as in German)
RONDE   RON-de
SOLVEIG   SOL-vay ('ay' as in 'hay')
VJALFELD   VYAL-fell

Note

This text went to press before the opening night, and may therefore differ slightly from the text as performed.

PART ONE

1.

A wooded slope near ÅSE'*s farm. A stream runs nearby. On the other side, an old mill. Hot summer day.* PEER GYNT *(sturdy; 20 years old) comes down the path. His mother* ÅSE *(small, slightly built) runs crossly after him, scolding him.*

ÅSE. Peer, you're lying.

PEER. I'm not, Ma.

ÅSE. Right then, swear.

PEER. Why should I?

ÅSE. It's a pack of lies!

PEER (*stopping*). Every blessed word's the truth.

ÅSE (*confronting him*). Aren't you ashamed? Your own mother! You choose the busiest time of year. You say you're going reindeer hunting. You're away for months. You come home in rags. No game. No gun. Are you going to open your eyes wide and spin me some tale about the one that got away? Well? Where did you see that reindeer?

PEER. Gjendin Ridge. The west side.

ÅSE (*scornfully*).   Really?

PEER. How the wind howled! I was sheltering
By some boulders. Then I heard him,
In the trees, beside the snowdrift,
Scraping moss.

ÅSE (*as before*). I don't believe it.

PEER. Shh! I held my breath. I heard him
Scraping, saw his antlers branching.
Carefully, I wriggled closer,
Squirmed across the rocks – and saw him

Clear as day, from round a boulder.
What a monster! Fat and glossy...
Ma, you'll never see his equal.

ÅSE. That I *do* believe.

PEER.   I fired then.
Down the deer fell on the hillside –
And the instant that he stumbled
Up I jumped, on to his shoulders,
Gripped him firmly by the left ear,
Drew my knife to slice his windpipe –
Hey! the ugly brute starts screaming,
Jumps up, sends my dagger flying,
Sheath and all. I'm caught. His antlers
Pin my legs, as tight as pincers.
Off he goes – his stride's enormous! -
Bounds along the ridge of Gjendin.

ÅSE (*involuntarily*). Lord have mercy!

PEER.   You know Gjendin.
Half a mile or more it stretches,
Sharp as a scythe. You're on the summit,
Looking down, this side or that side:
Gullies, sheer grey fells, and glaciers,
Till your eyes plunge into water,
Dark, deep water, half a mile below.

ÅSE (*swaying*). God save me!

PEER. All at once – there was no warning -
From the nest where it was huddling
On the eyebrow of the clifftop,
Flew a ptarmigan, wings flapping,
Startled, screeching. Hoo! The reindeer
Bounded skywards, turning, plunging
Down to the abyss below.

   ÅSE *totters and grasps a tree for support.* PEER *continues.*

At our backs, sheer cliff. Below us,
Emptiness. Through the mist we hurtled,
Startled seagulls, sent them spinning,
Wheeling, screaming, far below us.
Down and down and down we hurtled,
Till, below, a whitish glimmer,

Glistening like a reindeer's belly –
Ma, it was our own reflection,
Mirrored in the lake below us,
Rearing up as fast towards us
As we plunged madly, wildly down.

ÅSE (*panting*). Peer! In God's name, tell me quickly!

PEER. Deer from air and deer from water
Merged together in an instant,
Crashed and splashed and sent foam flying.
On he swam, with me astride him,
Going north, until he struggled,
Safe and sound, to shore. Then I came home.

ÅSE. But what about the deer?

PEER. He'll still be where I left him.

Snaps his fingers.

If you find him, you can keep him!

ÅSE. You didn't break your neck? Your legs?
Your back's all right? O God be praised
For saving him! It's true, you've torn
Your trousers. But who cares about that?
When I think what could have happened
In a leap like that...

She breaks off, looks at him wide-eyed and open-mouthed, can at first find nothing to say, then bursts out:

You lying devil! God in heaven, how you can lie! I thought I'd heard that tale before. I've known it since I was twenty. It happened to Gudbrand Glesne in the fairy story, not to you.

PEER. Must everything happen only once?

ÅSE (*in tears*). Oh God, I wish I was dead, asleep in the black ground! What does he care for prayers and tears? You're good for nothing, Peer. You always have been.

PEER. Ma, dear, sweetheart, all you say is true. Don't cry.

ÅSE. Leave me alone! How could I be happy – even if I wanted – with a pig of a son like you? Why shouldn't I cry, a poor widow, alone, ashamed? (*Weeping again.*) What's happened to all the happiness your granpa left us? Where are old Rasmus' moneybags? Your father sent them scampering, spilling gold like sand. The land he bought! The golden coach he rode in! That winter banquet, where every guest had his own glass and bottle, and smashed them against the wall!

PEER. Where are the snows of yesteryear?

ÅSE. Don't interrupt! Look at the farmhouse: windows stuffed with rags, fences broken, cattle outdoors in wind and storm, fields overgrown, every month another bailiff –

PEER. We've had bad luck before. It's always got better.

ÅSE. Salt's been sown where once our luck grew. Peer, you never change. You were always a stuck up brat. D'you remember the time that parson from Copenhagen asked your name, told you how princes, where he came from, would be glad of such airs and graces? Your Pa gave him a horse and a sledge for those kind words. Ah, those were the days! Parsons, captains, folk like that calling every day, stuffing themselves at our expense. Fair weather friends! The minute the goose was dead, everyone vanished. The place has been a desert ever since.

She wipes her eyes on her apron.

You're big. You're strong. You should be working hard on your inheritance. Your poor old mother's prop and stay!

In tears again.

Good for nothing! What help have you ever been to me? When you're in, you laze by the fire, poking and prodding the embers. When you're out you make girls shriek at dances or fight bigger wastrels than yourself. I'm so ashamed –

PEER (*moving away from her*). Leave me alone.

ÅSE (*going after him*). You mean it wasn't you started that punchup at Lunde? Everyone fighting like a pack of dogs! It wasn't you broke Blacksmith Aslak's arm? Well, fractured his finger, whatever it was you did.

PEER. Who told you such rubbish?

ÅSE (*crossly*). The whole street heard. Such howls!

PEER (*rubbing his elbow*). Oh yes. My howls.

ÅSE. What?

PEER. Yes, Ma. I was howling.

ÅSE. What d'you mean?

PEER. He's bigger than me. I've got marks to prove it.

ÅSE. Shame on you! Shame! You're no son of mine! You let that
drunk, that bully, that good for nothing . . . ? You let him . . . ?

She bursts into tears again.

Haven't I enough to bear? This is the worst of all. Just because
he's bigger than you, you *let* him beat you up?

PEER. It's all right, Ma.

ÅSE. Why? Was that another lie?

PEER. Yes. Do stop crying.

He clenches his left fist.

> See: I held him in these pincers,
> Bent him over, bent him double,
> Gave that blacksmith such a thrashing –

ÅSE. Another thrashing! You'll be the death of me.

PEER. No, Ma. Darling. Sweetheart. Cabbage.
All I have. You're all I cherish.
Trust me. Word of honour. One day
Everyone in town will bow to
Åse Gynt, Peer's mother, mother
Of Peer who did the mighty deed.

ÅSE (*snorting*). You?

PEER.   Who else? Who knows the future?

ÅSE. Who knows if you'll learn enough to patch those pants?

PEER (*hotly*). I'll be a king, a Kaiser.

ÅSE. You're crazy. Mind you . . . you could have been someone,
if you hadn't been such a liar. That girl at Haegstad fancied
you. If you'd played your cards right, you could have won that
game.

PEER. You think so?

ÅSE (*weeping again*). Oh Peer, just think of it. The dowry! The
old man's heir! You could have been dancing at your own
wedding, instead of standing here in rags.

PEER (*eagerly*). I'll do it.

ÅSE. What?

PEER. Ask him at Haegstad.

ÅSE. Oh Peer! You can't. Not any more.

PEER. Why not?

ÅSE. You're too late. I might have known.

PEER. What d'you mean?

ÅSE (*sobbing*). While you were riding reindeers, he promised her to Mads Moen.

PEER. Mads Moen? That idiot?

ÅSE. He's going to marry her.

PEER. Wait here. I'll fetch the cart.

He starts to go.

ÅSE. The wedding's tomorrow.

PEER. Doesn't matter. I'll go tonight.

ÅSE. Don't people laugh at us enough? You'll make things worse.

PEER. No, Ma. This time luck's on our side.
     Look! Who needs a horse and cart?

Laughing and shouting together, he picks her up.

No time to waste in harnessing!

ÅSE. Put me down!

PEER. I'll take you to the wedding. I'll carry you!

He wades into the stream.

ÅSE. Lord have mercy! Peer! We'll drown!

PEER. I wasn't born for drowning.

ÅSE. You were born to be hanged!

She pulls his hair.

Pig! Put me down!

PEER. Stop wriggling. The bottom's slippery here.

ÅSE. Donkey!

PEER. Nag all you like. That won't trip us up. Ah, the bottom's sloping.

ÅSE. Don't let go!

PEER. Hey-up! Hey-a! Peer and the reindeer!

Prancing about.

I'm the reindeer. You be Peer.

ÅSE. I don't know what I'm meant to be!

PEER. It's shallow now.

He wades to shore.

There. Give your horsey a great big kiss.

ÅSE *boxes his ears.*

ÅSE. Put me down!

PEER. I'll take you to the wedding first. You're clever. You talk for me. Talk to the old fool. Tell him Mads Moen is a drunk –

ÅSE. Down!

PEER. Tell him the sort of man Peer Gynt is.

ÅSE. I'll do that all right. I'll leave nothing out. Every trick, every lie.

PEER. You're joking.

ÅSE (*kicking him in her fury*). I won't stop till the old man sets his dogs on you, like the pig you are!

PEER. I think I'll leave you here.

ÅSE. I'll get there on my own.

PEER. Don't be daft! You're not strong enough.

ÅSE. I could crunch millstones. I could splinter flints. Put me down!

PEER. If you promise.

ÅSE. No! I'm going with you, and they're going to hear the sort of man you are.

PEER. You're staying here.

ÅSE. I'm going with you.

PEER. Don't bet on it.

ÅSE. What are you going to do?

PEER. I'm putting you on the millhouse roof. Sit there.

He puts her on the roof. ÅSE *shrieks.*

ÅSE. Lift me down!

PEER. Only if you listen.

ÅSE. Pah!

PEER. Ma, sweetheart, listen . . .

ÅSE. Lift me down at once!

She throws a lump of turf at him.

PEER. I daren't.

He goes closer.

Sit still. Don't wriggle. You'll fall and hurt yourself.

ÅSE. Pig!

PEER. Careful.

ÅSE. I'll give you such a thrashing. You're not too big.

PEER. Goodbye, Ma. Wait there. I won't be long.

He goes, then turns, wags his finger at her and says:

Mind you don't fall!

He goes.

ÅSE. Peer! God in heaven, he's gone. Reindeer rider! Liar!
Listen to me! No, he's away across the fields. (*Shrieking.*)
Help! I'm giddy!

Two WOMEN, *carrying grain sacks, come down towards the mill.*

FIRST WOMAN. Who's that shouting?

ÅSE. Me!

SECOND WOMAN. Åse! What are you doing up there?

ÅSE. Bring a ladder. Get me down. That devil Peer –

FIRST WOMAN. You mean your own son . . . ?

ÅSE. Help me down. I've got to get to Haegstad.

SECOND WOMAN. Is that where he is?

FIRST WOMAN. He'll be sorry. The smith went that way too.

ÅSE (*wringing her hands*). God help me! My poor boy! They'll murder him!

FIRST WOMAN. Right enough. I know that crowd.

SECOND WOMAN. That was a daft thing to say. (*Shouts up the hill*). Eivind! Anders! Come and help!

MAN'S VOICE. What's up?

SECOND WOMAN. Peer Gynt's put his mother on the roof!

2.

A hillside covered with heather and bushes. Upstage: the road, divided from us by a fence. PEER *comes along a path, hurries to the fence, stands and looks at the view beyond.*

PEER. Down over yonder. That's Haegstad. Not far now.

He climbs half over the fence, then stops.

I wonder if Ingrid's inside, all alone?

He shields his eyes and looks more closely.

No.
Guests in the farmyard, all buzzing like midges,
Loaded with presents. I'm wasting my time here.

He climbs back over the fence, and begins absent-mindedly pulling leaves from the bushes.

Oh, I could do with a drink. Can I slip down
Quickly, before someone sees me who knows me?
No, a big drink would be best. They could laugh then
Hard as they liked, and I'd not even notice.

All at once he starts, looks round and hides in the bushes. Some PEOPLE, *carrying presents, go along the road to the wedding. They are deep in conversation.*

A MAN. His Pa was a drunk, and his mother's not strong.

A WOMAN. Hardly surprising the boy's such a failure.

They pass, and soon afterwards PEER *comes out. He is blushing with shame, and looks after them.*

PEER (*quietly*). Me? That was me they were talking of?

He gives an exaggerated shrug.

Well, sticks and stones! Let them say what they like!

He sprawls down on a bank of heather, lies on his back with his hands behind his head, and gazes up into the sky.

What an odd-looking cloud. It's like a horse. There's the rider . . . the saddle . . . the harness. Behind it, a witch on a broomstick. (*Smiling to himself.*) It's Ma. She's yelling: 'Peer! Hey! Peer, you pig!'.

Little by little he closes his eyes.

She's scared now, all right.
Peer rides in state at the head of his column.
Gold are his horseshoes, his harness is silver.
Fine leather gauntlets. A sabre. A scabbard.
Uniform coat, lined with silk, ankle-length.
Handsome the soldiers who follow his footsteps;
Not one can equal him, proud on his charger,
Dazzling, outglittering all in the sunshine.
Lining the roadside, the people stand gaping,
Touching their caps as they gaze up in wonder.
Women drop curtseys. It's Peer Gynt, the Kaiser,
Leading his vassals – a thousand! – in triumph.
Ducats and guineas and golden half-sovereigns
Sprinkle the roadway as if they were pebbles.
Look! Every subject's as rich as a lord!
Peer gallops over the wavetips in glory.
Engelland's prince on the seashore is waiting,
Engelland's maidens all eager beside him.
Engelland's nobles and Engelland's Kaiser
Rise to their feet as our hero approaches.
Tipping his coronet, Engelland's Kaiser says –

ASLAK (*as he and some other* PEOPLE *pass by on the path above*). Hey, Peer Gynt, you drunken swine.

PEER (*half awake*). Pardon, milord?

ASLAK (*leaning on the fence, grinning*). Time to get up, little fellow.

PEER. Aslak! What do you want?

ASLAK (*to the others*). Still groggy after Lunde!

PEER (*jumping up*). Get stuffed!

ASLAK. Where the hell have you been, these last six weeks? Did
the trolls get you?

PEER. You wouldn't believe where I've been, Aslak.

ASLAK (*winking at the others*). Oh Peer, do tell.

PEER. Forget it.

ASLAK (*after a short pause*). Going to Haegstad, are you?

PEER. No.

ASLAK. People said that girl there fancied you.

PEER. You bastard –

ASLAK (*drawing back a little*). Keep your hair on. Even if she's
not interested, there are plenty of others. What? John Gynt's
son? Come to the wedding. They'll be flocks of them:
lambkins, tough old ewes...

PEER. Go to hell!

ASLAK. There'll be someone there who fancies you. Bye, then.
I'll kiss the bride for you.

They go, laughing and whistling. PEER *looks after them for a
moment, then turns with a shrug.*

PEER. She can marry who she likes. See if I care.

He looks down at his clothes.

Torn trousers. Patches. Rags. I wish I'd a new suit. (*Stamping
in rage.*) If I'd only been a butcher! I'd cut their laughing
throats!

He starts and looks round.

What's that? Someone laughing? I thought I... Nobody. Ah,
I'm going home to Ma.

*He goes to the gate, then stands and listens, in the direction of the
wedding.*

They're dancing!

He stares and listens, moves towards the fence. His eyes gleam; he rubs his palms on his thighs.

What a crowd of girls! Seven or eight per man. Hell and damnation, I've got to go. But what about Ma, sitting up there on the mill roof?

His eyes are drawn to the wedding again. He laughs and does a few dance steps.

They're dancing a halling. That's Guttorm playing. Listen to it, leaping like a waterfall! Think of the girls...the glowing, glittering girls. Hell and damnation, I've got to go!

He jumps over the fence and hurries off down the road.

3.

Courtyard at Haegstad, in front of the farm buildings. Many guests. Lively dancing on the lawn. The FIDDLER *sits on a table; the* STEWARD *stands in the doorway.* SERVING MAIDS *go back and forth from building to building.* OLD PEOPLE *sit here and there, gossiping. A* WOMAN *joins a group of* GUESTS, *sitting on some logs.*

WOMAN. The bride? Well, of course she's crying. What d'you expect?

STEWARD (*in another group*). Drink up, everyone!

MADS, *the bridegroom, goes to his* FATHER, *who is talking to a group of* GUESTS. *He whimpers and pulls his* FATHER*'s sleeve.*

MADS. She won't, Pa. She just won't.

FATHER. Won't what?

MADS. She's locked herself in.

FATHER. So find the key.

MADS. I don't know where to look.

FATHER. What a dummy!

He turns back to the others. MADS *wanders across the yard. A* YOUNG MAN *calls from behind the house.*

YOUNG MAN. Hey up, girls! Peer Gynt's arrived.

ASLAK (*who has just come onstage*). Who invited him?

STEWARD (*as he goes towards the house*). No one.

ASLAK (*to the* GIRLS). Whatever he says, pretend you don't hear.

A GIRL (*to the others*). Pretend you don't even see him!

PEER GYNT *comes in, eager and excited. He claps his hands.*

PEER. Which of you girls knows how to dance?

A GIRL (*nearest to him*). Not me.

ANOTHER (*the same*). Not me.

ANOTHER. I don't.

PEER (*to a fourth*). How about you?

THE GIRL (*turning away*). I'm just going home.

PEER. So soon? You're crazy!

ASLAK (*after a pause, softly*). Oh look, Peer, she's dancing with that old man.

PEER *turns quickly to an older man.*

PEER. Where are the girls who want to dance?

OLDER MAN (*turning away*). Keep looking.

PEER *is somewhat taken aback. He looks sidelong, embarrassed at the* GUESTS. *They look at him, but no one speaks. He goes towards one group after another. Wherever he goes, there is sudden silence; when he moves on, people smirk after him. He drags his hand along the railing.* SOLVEIG, *holding* LITTLE HELGA *by the hand, follows her parents into the yard.*

GUEST (*to someone close to* PEER). It's the strangers from Heldal.

PEER *goes to meet the newcomers. He gestures to* SOLVEIG *and speaks to her father.*

PEER. May I dance with your daughter?

SOLVEIG'S FATHER (*stopping*). Yes. But first we must go inside, and say hello.

They go in. The STEWARD *offers* PEER *a drink.*

STEWARD. As long as you're here, you'd better wet your whistle.

PEER (*gazing after the newcomers*). No thanks. I'm not thirsty. I'm going to dance.

The STEWARD *goes.* PEER *looks towards the house, and laughs.*

> What a picture! What a sight to see!
> Downcast eyes . . . snowy white apron . . . hand
> Clasping her mother's skirts . . . prayer book wrapped
> In a kerchief . . . I must go in and see.

He goes towards the house, but is met by a group of YOUNG MEN *coming out.*

YOUNG MAN. Peer! Tired of dancing already?

PEER. No.

YOUNG MAN. You're going the wrong way, then.

He takes him by the shoulders and turns him round.

PEER. Let go.

YOUNG MAN. Scared of Aslak, are you?

PEER. Me, scared?

YOUNG MAN. Remember what happened at Lunde!

The YOUNG MEN *laugh and go to join the dancing.* SOLVEIG *stands in the doorway.*

SOLVEIG. Are you the young man who asked for a dance?

PEER. Yes. Can't you tell? Come on!

He takes her hand.

SOLVEIG. Not too far away, Ma says.

PEER. Ma says? Ma says? How old are you?

SOLVEIG. Don't laugh.

PEER. You're just a baby. You are old enough...?

SOLVEIG. I was confirmed last spring.

PEER. What's your name?

SOLVEIG. Solveig. What's yours?

PEER. Peer Gynt.

SOLVEIG *pulls her hand from his.*

SOLVEIG. My God!

PEER. What's the matter now?

SOLVEIG. My garter's slipping. I must go in and fasten it.

She goes. MADS *comes by, pulling his* MOTHER's *sleeve.*

MADS. Ma, she won't.

MADS' MOTHER. Won't what?

MADS. Just won't.

MADS' MOTHER. What?

MADS. Unlock her door to me.

MADS' FATHER (*aside to him, furious*). You ought to be locked in the stable!

MADS' MOTHER. Poor darling! Leave him alone. He'll manage.

They go. A group of YOUNG PEOPLE *come from among the dancers.*

YOUNG MAN. Swig of brandy, Peer?

PEER. No.

YOUNG MAN. Just a mouthful?

PEER (*looking darkly at him*). Have you got some?

YOUNG MAN. Maybe.

He drinks from a pocket flask.

Kicks like a horse. Want some?

PEER. Let me.

He drinks.

SECOND YOUNG MAN. Try mine now.

PEER. No.

SECOND YOUNG MAN. Don't be an idiot. Try it!

PEER. Just a drop.

He drinks.

A GIRL (*in a low voice*). Come on, let's go.

PEER. What's the matter, Miss? Are you afraid of me?

THIRD YOUNG MAN. Who isn't afraid of you?

FOURTH YOUNG MAN. We all know what you did at Lunde.

PEER. That was nothing. If I really lost my temper...

FIRST YOUNG MAN (*whispering*). He's hooked!

SEVERAL (*round him in a circle*). What? What? What would you
   do?

PEER. I'll tell you tomorrow.

OTHERS. Now! Tonight!

A GIRL. Can you put spells on people, Peer?

PEER. I can raise the Devil.

YOUNG MAN. My Granny could do that before I was born.

PEER. Liar! No one else can do what I can do.
    I squeezed him into a nutshell once.
    In through a wormhole.

YOUNG PEOPLE (*laughing*). Of course you did!

PEER. He cursed and cried and swore he'd give
    Me all I asked.

YOUNG MAN.   And still you pushed?

PEER. I rammed him in and plugged the hole.
    Hoo! How he buzzed and roared.

GIRL.   Just fancy!

PEER. Yes. Buzzed just like a bumblebee.

GIRL. You've got him still, inside the nut?

PEER. No. He got clean away. In fact,
    My quarrel with Aslak's all his fault.

YOUNG MAN. Why's that?

PEER. I took him to Aslak, in the nut,
    And asked the smith to break the shell.
    He said he would. He put it on the anvil,
    Then – you know Aslak – wallop! Bang!
    He smashed that nut to smithereens.

A VOICE FROM THE CROWD. And walloped the Devil down
to hell?

PEER. Of course not. Well, he did his best,
But the Devil did better: turned himself
To a fiery flame and slipped away
Through ceiling and solid wall.

SEVERAL.   And Aslak?

PEER. Ha! You know Aslak. Scorched himself.
Since then we've not been best of friends.

Laughter.

SOME GUESTS. What a story!

OTHERS. His best yarn yet!

PEER. You think I made it up?

YOUNG MAN. Oh no. Not you. I heard it years ago from
Granpa.

PEER. Liar! It happened to me! I can saddle my charger and
ride the stars. I can...do anything I like.

More laughter.

A VOICE. Go on, Peer. Ride the stars!

VOICES. Go on, Peer. Ride!

PEER. Like a storm, one day I'll ride you down. The whole pack
of you. Then you'll tremble!

AN OLDER MAN. He's off his head.

ANOTHER. Fool!

ANOTHER. Babbler!

ANOTHER. Liar!

PEER (*squaring up to them*). Wait and see!

DRUNK. *You* wait. I'll mash you, mate.

VOICES. Mash! Bash! Thrash!

The crowd breaks up, the OLDER GUESTS *angry, the* YOUNG
PEOPLE *laughing and jeering.* MADS MOEN *goes up to* PEER.

MADS. Peer, is it true you can ride the stars?

PEER (*curtly*). Anything you like. Just say the word.

MADS. You've got a hat of invisibility?

PEER. A cloak, you mean? Of course.

He turns from him, as SOLVEIG *and* HELGA *cross the yard, hand in hand.* PEER *runs to them, radiant.*

Solveig! Thank God you've come!

He takes her wrist.

Now I'll show you how I dance.

SOLVEIG. Let go.

PEER. Why?

SOLVEIG. You're mad.

PEER. Mad as a reindeer when summer comes! Hurry up. Don't sulk.

SOLVEIG (*pulling away*). I daren't.

PEER. Why not?

SOLVEIG. You're drunk.

She moves away with HELGA.

PEER. I should have knifed the whole pack of them!

MADS (*plucking his elbow*). Can't you help me? I can't get in.

PEER (*thoughtfully*). Locked you out, has she? Where?

MADS. In the hayloft.

PEER. Really?

MADS. Come on, Peer. Help me!

PEER. No. You should have asked before.

A thought strikes him. He says softly and with meaning:

The bride. Ingrid. In the hayloft.

He goes to SOLVEIG.

Well? Have you decided?

SOLVEIG *tries to go, but he bars her way.*

It's because I'm in rags. You're afraid of me.

SOLVEIG (*quickly*). It isn't that.

PEER. It is. And because I'm a little drunk. That was to spite
  you, when you hurt me. Come on.

SOLVEIG. I daren't. Even if I wanted to.

PEER. Who are you scared of?

SOLVEIG. Pa, most of all.

PEER. Your father. Oh yes. The kneeler. The psalm singer.
  That's right, isn't it? Isn't he?

SOLVEIG. Isn't he what?

PEER. A preacher. Our father the preacher. And you and your
  mother? Are you goody-goody too?

SOLVEIG. Leave me alone.

PEER. No!

  He puts on a low, sinister voice.

> I'll turn into a troll. At night I'll come.
> As midnight strikes. You'll hear a hsss! a fsss!
> It's not the cat you hear. It's me. I'll drain
> Your blood in a cup. And little sister, too,
> I'll eat her too. At night the werewolf feasts.
> I'll gnaw your flesh. I'll crunch your bones.

  He changes his tone again, and beseeches her like a man in agony.

  Oh Solveig, dance with me.

SOLVEIG (*making a face at him*). You're horrible!

  She goes into the house. MADS *makes his way to* PEER *again.*

MADS. I'll give you an ox, if you help me.

PEER. Come on!

  They go round the back of the house. At the same moment a crowd of
  GUESTS *come back from dancing, most of them drunk. Confusion.*
  SOLVEIG, HELGA *and their* PARENTS, *with a group of older*
  GUESTS, *come to the door. The* STEWARD *goes to* ASLAK, *who is*
  at the forefront of the hubbub.

STEWARD. Be quiet!

ASLAK (*taking off his coat*). No. It's got to be settled, here and
  now. Either Peer Gynt or I gets thrashed.

SOME GUESTS. Fight! Fight!

OTHER GUESTS. Talk! Don't fight.

ASLAK. No talking. Fighting.

SOLVEIG'S FATHER. Be quiet, you fool.

ASLAK (*throwing down his coat*). I'll murder him!

SOLVEIG'S MOTHER (*to* SOLVEIG). You see what they think of him? Your halfwit!

ÅSE *comes in, brandishing a stick.*

ÅSE. Is my son here? He's going to smart! I'm going to thrash him black and blue.

ASLAK (*rolling up his shirtsleeves*). Not you. You're far too frail.

GUESTS. Let Aslak thrash him.

OTHERS. Bash him!

OTHERS. Smash him!

ASLAK (*spitting on his hands and nodding to* ÅSE). String him up!

ÅSE. What? String up my Peer? Just try. We'll show you a thing or two. Where is he?

She calls across the yard.

Peer!

MADS *runs in.*

MADS. Oh God! Help! Ma! Pa! Ohhhhh!

MADS' FATHER. What's wrong?

MADS. Peer Gynt! He's –

ÅSE (*screaming*). No! You've killed him! Oh!

MADS. No no. Peer Gynt, he's . . . look, up there.

VOICES. With the bride.

ÅSE (*lowering her stick*). That devil!

ASLAK (*as if thunderstruck*). Climbing the highest fell. Like a mountain goat.

MADS (*in tears*). He's carrying her! Ma! He's carrying her like a puppy dog!

ÅSE (*shaking her fist at* PEER). I hope you fall and –

   She shrieks with apprehension.

   Do be careful!

   The BRIDE'S FATHER *comes out, bareheaded and white with rage.*

BRIDE'S FATHER. He took my daughter! I'll murder him!

ÅSE. In God's name, no! Take me! Take me!

4.

A narrow path, high in the hills. Early morning. PEER *hurries in, followed by* INGRID. *She is still wearing some of her bride's finery, and is trying to hold him back.*

PEER. Go away.

INGRID (*in tears*). After what happened? Where to?

PEER. Anywhere you like.

INGRID. There's nothing here. Just hills and snow.

PEER. See if I care.

INGRID (*wringing her hands*). You lied to me.

PEER. Stop whining. We've got to part.

INGRID. After what we did . . . ?

PEER. To Hell with it! To Hell with women – all but one.

INGRID. Which one?

PEER. Not you.

INGRID. Who?

PEER. Go away! Go home to Daddy!

INGRID. Darling –

PEER. That's enough.

INGRID. You don't mean it.

PEER. Yes I do.

INGRID. After all you promised...

PEER. What can you give me?

INGRID. The farm at Haegstad. And . . . other things.

PEER. Where's the prayer book in your kerchief? Where are
   your golden curls? Do you look modestly down at your apron
   . . . hold your mother's skirt? Well, do you?

INGRID. No, I –

PEER. Were you confirmed last spring?

INGRID. No, but –

PEER. Do you blush and look bashful? Do you turn me down?

INGRID. Lord, he's raving!

PEER. Who feels holy when he sees you?

INGRID. Peer, I –

PEER. So why should I care for the rest of it?

   He turns to go. INGRID *stops him.*

INGRID. If you leave me after this, they'll hang you.

PEER. Let them.

INGRID. You could be rich, looked up to. Marry me -

PEER. No.

INGRID (*bursting into tears*). You tricked me.

PEER. You let me.

INGRID. I was unhappy.

PEER. I was crazy.

INGRID (*threateningly*). You'll be sorry.

PEER. Don't bet on it.

INGRID. You won't change your mind?

PEER. No chance.

INGRID. Right. We'll see who wins.

   She goes down the hill. PEER *stands for a moment, then suddenly
   shouts:*

To Hell with it! To Hell with women!

INGRID (*mockingly, turning and calling back*). All but one.

PEER. All but one.

They go, in opposite directions.

5.

By a tarn, high in the hills. Bog and moor all round. A storm blowing up. ÅSE, in despair, is searching and calling everywhere. SOLVEIG only just keeps up with her. SOLVEIG's PARENTS and HELGA follow, some way behind. ÅSE is windmilling her arms and tearing her hair.

ÅSE. The world's in a rage. The world's against him.
  Sky, water, the hateful hills!
  Sky sends fog to baffle him.
  Water smiles, and laps, and drowns.
  Hills topple and slide. And all those people!
  Out to hang him. No, God, no!
  I need him. Oh, the fool,
  To let the Devil tempt him so!

She turns to SOLVEIG.

Who'd have believed such a thing could happen? He was a
talker, a daydreamer. But that's all he was. He never *did*
anything. I don't know whether to laugh or cry.
  We were so close. In all our troubles.
  You understand, his Pa drank –
  Ran round joking, gossiping,
  Played 'Catch!' with our inheritance.
  Me and Peerkin sat at home,
  Trying to take no notice. What else could we do?
  I didn't dare face facts –
  It's so hard to watch your own fate
  Creeping up on you. You try not to look.
  You try not to think. Some drown
  Their sorrows. Some turn to lies.
  Me and Peer chose fairy tales.
  Princes . . . trolls . . . magic animals . . .

Yes, and stolen brides. Who'd have thought
That the Devil would stick
Such fancies in his mind for good?

Terrified again.

What was that? A water sprite, a will o' the wisp! Peer! Peer!
Up there...

She runs to the top of a small rise and looks out over the tarn.
SOLVEIG's PARENTS *join her.*

No sign.

SOLVEIG'S FATHER (*softly*). It's looking bad.

ÅSE. Oh, Peer! My own lost lamb.

SOLVEIG'S FATHER (*nodding gently*). Lost indeed.

ÅSE. Don't say that! He's so clever. There's none like him.

SOLVEIG'S FATHER. Foolish woman.

ÅSE. Oh yes! I'm the fool. There's nothing wrong with him.

SOLVEIG'S FATHER (*always quietly and with gentle eyes*). His
heart is stone. His soul is lost.

ÅSE (*terrified*). How could God do that?

SOLVEIG'S FATHER. Does he bend with the burden of his sin?

ÅSE (*eagerly*). He saddles a reindeer and rides the sky.

SOLVEIG'S MOTHER. You're mad.

SOLVEIG'S FATHER. What are you saying?

ÅSE. Nothing's too hard for him. You'll see.

SOLVEIG'S FATHER. I think we'll see him hang.

ÅSE (*shrieking*). God have mercy!

SOLVEIG'S FATHER. Perhaps he'll repent when he sees the
executioner.

ÅSE (*confused*). I don't know what you mean. My head swims.
We must find him.

SOLVEIG'S FATHER. We must save his soul.

ÅSE. And his body! If he's in the marsh, we'll drag him out. If trolls have taken him, we'll ring the bells.

SOLVEIG'S FATHER. Ah! Here's a track.

ÅSE. God reward you for helping me!

SOLVEIG'S FATHER. It's our Christian duty.

ÅSE. The rest are heathens. None offered to come and look.

SOLVEIG'S FATHER. They know him too well.

ÅSE. He was far too good for them.

She wrings her hands.

And now he's in danger. Deadly danger.

SOLVEIG'S FATHER. Here's a footprint.

ÅSE. We're on the right track.

SOLVEIG'S FATHER. Spread out. We'll look down there.

He and SOLVEIG'*s* MOTHER *go.*

SOLVEIG (*to* ÅSE). Tell me some more.

ÅSE (*wiping her eyes*). About my son?

SOLVEIG. Yes. Everything.

ÅSE (*smiles and holds her head up proudly*). You'd grow tired of listening.

SOLVEIG. Oh no! You'd grow tired of telling first . . .

6.

Treeless, hilly country. Mountain tops in the distance. Evening: long shadows. PEER *runs in full tilt, and stops on the slope.*

PEER. They're all after me. Guns, sticks. Led by that old fool from Haegstad. The secret's out: Peer Gynt's on the run! This is better than pummelling that blacksmith. This is living! Every muscle as strong as a bear's!

He shadow boxes.

Bash! Crash! Hold back that waterfall! Tear up that tree! This is living! To hell with fairy tales!

Three HERDGIRLS *run over the hillsides, shouting and singing.*

HERDGIRLS. Trolls of the mountain! Trolls, cooee!
    Trolls of the hills! Come sleep with me!

PEER. Who are you shouting for?

HERDGIRLS. Trolls! Trolls! Trolls!

FIRST GIRL. Darling troll, be kind!

SECOND GIRL. Be rough!

THIRD GIRL. The beds in the hut are waiting.

FIRST GIRL. Kind is rough.

SECOND GIRL. And rough is kind.

THIRD GIRL. Trolls, cooee! Come sleep with me!

PEER. Where are your husbands? Your mortal men?

HERDGIRLS (*shrieking with laughter*). They never came!

FIRST GIRL. 'Darling', mine called me. 'Pussycat.' Now he's married to a ton of widow.

SECOND GIRL. Mine met a gipsy girl, far up north. Now they're tramping the road together.

THIRD GIRL. Mine took our bastard and cut his throat. Now his head stands grinning on a stake.

HERDGIRLS. Trolls of the mountain! Trolls, cooee!
    Trolls of the hills! Come sleep with me!

PEER *leaps suddenly among them.*

PEER. I'm a troll. Three-headed! A three-girl troll!

HERDGIRLS. Are you up to it?

PEER. Try me and see.

FIRST GIRL. To the hut! To the hut!

SECOND GIRL. We've mead to drink.

PEER. Let's drink!

THIRD GIRL. No empty beds tonight!

SECOND GIRL (*kissing* PEER). He glows like red-hot iron.

THIRD GIRL (*kissing him*). He leaps like a trout in a pool.

HERDGIRLS. Peer of the mountain! Peer cooee!
Peer of the hills! Come dance with me!

They surround PEER *and dance with him, away across the hills.*

7.

In the Ronde mountains. Sunset. Gleaming snowpeaks all round.
PEER *comes in, lost and confused.*

PEER. Castle on castle rising.
See where the gateway gleams.
Stop! Will you stop! It's moving,
Further and further away.
Cock on the weather vane flapping,
Fluttering, ready to fly.
Rock-drifts, mists and mirages.
The mountain is locked and barred.

Look there! Treeroots and branches,
High on the hilltops. What are they?
Warriors. Giants. Heron-footed –
Melting and merging. All gone now.

Rainbow-colours, shimmering,
Dazzling eyes and brain.
Bells in the distance. Pain,
Slung from my eyebrows,
Clamping my forehead,
A red-hot, glowing ring.
But which devil fastened it?
Can't remember. Can't remember.

He sinks down.

Flight over Gjendin –
Daydream and lies.
Climbing the fellside,
Bridenapping. Drunk.
Hunting with eagles,
Brawling with trolls,

Romping with madwomen –
Daydream and lies.

Pause. He gazes up.

Brown eagles, hovering,
Wild geese flying south.
Why must I stumble
Kneedeep in filth?

He jumps up.

I'll fly with them! I'll wash myself clean
In the wind-bath on high.
Soaring and swooping, I'll cleanse my sins
In the font of the sky.
Over the pastures, dipping and gliding,
Free as air!
Over the sea-swell, over his lordship
The crown prince of Engelland,
Standing there.
Gape at me, girls! Don't wait for me, girls!
My charger won't ride here again.
Well, perhaps just this once, for a moment . . .

What's happened? The eagles –
Some devil has snatched them away.

Look. See the gable-end, rising,
Stone by stone,
Building itself from the rubble.
Open door.
Ha! Now I know it! It's Granpa's
Farm, rebuilt.
Rags in the windows? All gone now.
Brand new fence.
Lights gleaming everywhere. Feasting,
There, inside.

What's that? Shh! The parson's
Tapping his knife on his glass.
The captain's hurling a bottle,
Smashing the mirror to pieces.
No, hush, Ma. Don't stop them.
There's plenty. Who cares about waste?
This is rich Johnny Gynt's dinner party –
Three cheers for the family of Gynt!

What was that? Such bustle! Such fuss now!
What's that yelling and shouting in aid of?
'Bring Peer!' cry the captain, the parson.
'Fill your glasses and drink up. To Peer!'
Peer Gynt, go inside. The announcement is made.
They'll proclaim it in music and song.
'Peer Gynt, to greatness you were born.
In greatness live, till the day you die!'

He jumps up and runs nosefirst into the rockface. He falls and lies still.

8.

Hillside. Tall, leafy trees, rustling. Stars twinkling through the leaves. Birds singing in the treetops. A WOMAN, *dressed in green, comes in.* PEER *follows her, the picture of someone sick with love. She stops and turns.*

WOMAN. Is that true?

PEER (*drawing a finger to cut his throat*). As true as I'm called Peer. As true as you're beautiful. Will you have me? You'll see how kind I'll be. You won't have to spin or weave. You'll eat fit to burst. I'll never pull your hair.

WOMAN. You won't hit me?

PEER. Of course not. We princes don't hit women.

WOMAN. You really are a prince?

PEER. Yep.

WOMAN. My father's a king. His castle's a mountain.

PEER. My mother's is bigger. Bound to be.

WOMAN. Have you heard of him? King Brose.

PEER. Have you heard of her? Queen Åse.

WOMAN. When he's angry, the mountains shake.

PEER. When she nags, they quake.

WOMAN. He dances like a dream.

PEER. She prances through the stream.

WOMAN. Do you always wear those rags?

PEER. You should see my Sunday bags.

WOMAN. I wear gold and silk each day.

PEER. Looks more like grass and hay.

WOMAN. Ah! You don't understand. That's our custom, here in the mountains. Nothing is what it seems. For example, when you come to my father's palace, you probably won't recognise it. You'll think it's a rubble-heap.

PEER. It's just the same with us! You'd probably think our gold was rust and dust. You'd think our windows were stuffed with rags and socks.

WOMAN. Black looks white, and short looks tall.

PEER. Foul looks fair, and big looks small.

The WOMAN *throws her arms round his neck.*

WOMAN. Oh Peer, we belong together!

PEER. Like foot and shoe; like hair and comb.

WOMAN (*calling across the hillside*). Grane! Grane! (*To* PEER.) My wedding steed.

A gigantic pig lollops in, bridled with a length of rope and saddled with a sack. PEER *swings on to its back and takes the* WOMAN *in front of him.*

PEER. Hi-yoh! We'll gallop inside in style.
   Giddy-ap! Horse in a million! Ho!

WOMAN (*seductively*). And to think I was feeling sad.
   You never can tell. You never can tell.

PEER *beats the pig until it trots out.*

PEER. You can tell a prince by the steed he rides!

9.

Hall of the OLD MAN OF THE MOUNTAIN. *Crowds of courtiers:*
TROLLS, GNOMES, GOBLINS. *The* OLD MAN *enthroned, with
crown and sceptre. His* CHILDREN *and* RELATIONS *on either side.*
PEER *stands before him. Uproar.*

TROLLS. Kill him! Princess-snatcher! Christian! Liar!

FIRST TROLL CHILD. Let me slice his fingers.

SECOND TROLL CHILD. Let me rip his hair.

TROLL MAIDEN. Let me bite his bum.

FIRST TROLL OLD WOMAN (*with a ladle*). Boil him for soup!

SECOND TROLL OLD WOMAN (*with a cleaver*). Slice him and
stew him!

OLD MAN. Cool! Ice cool!

He beckons his courtiers nearer.

Keep tight control. These last few years, we've not been doing
so well. Our future's uncertain. When human help arrives, we
shouldn't kick it away. Also, this is a fine specimen. Almost
unblemished. Pretty well put together. Granted, just one
head. But so's my daughter. Three-headers are right out of
fashion, and two-headers – when you see them nowadays –
aren't worth the trip. (*To* PEER.) Fancy my daughter, do you?

PEER. And a kingdom for dowry, yes.

OLD MAN. Half now, the rest when I fall off the perch.

PEER. Done.

OLD MAN. Hang on. This is two-way trade. If your face doesn't
fit, you don't get out alive. Number One, promises. You give
up everything outside this kingdom. No more daylight. No
more . . . sun and games.

PEER. To be called king, it's worth it.

OLD MAN. Number Two, intelligence test.

He rises from the throne.

AN ANCIENT TROLL, THE CHAMBERLAIN (*to* PEER). How
are your wisdom teeth? Will you crack the Old Man's riddle?

OLD MAN. Trolls and humans – what's the difference?

PEER. None that I can see. Little trolls want to maul you, big trolls want to skewer you. Give humans half a chance, we'd do the same.

OLD MAN. I like it. But morning's morning. Evening's evening. We're chalk and cheese. I'll tell you. Out there, where the sky shines, humans say: 'To thyself be true'. In here, trolls say: 'Be true to yourself – ish'.

CHAMBERLAIN (*to* PEER). D'you get it?

PEER. Dimly.

OLD MAN. 'Ish'. Finest letters in the alphabet. Paint them on your buckler, son in law.

PEER (*scratching his head*). But –

OLD MAN. D'you want to be king?

PEER. Ah. Finest letters. Right.

OLD MAN. Number Three. You learn to enjoy our simple, homely lifestyle.

He beckons. Two pig-headed TROLLS, *wearing white nightcaps, bring in food and drink.*

Cow-cakes. Bull-beer. Never mind if they're too sweet or too sour. They're local produce. That's the main thing.

PEER (*pushing them away*). Take the bloody things away. I'll never get used to this.

OLD MAN. No food, no girl.

PEER (*thoughtfully*). H'm. 'What can't be cured . . .' Maybe it's not so sour. Bottoms up!

He drinks.

OLD MAN. Good. Hey, are you spitting?

PEER. Force of habit.

OLD MAN. Next, get rid of those Christian clothes. It's the way we do things here. Local materials. Nothing imported – except the silk bow on the end of your tail.

PEER (*crossly*). I haven't got a tail.

OLD MAN. No problem. Chamberlain, my Sunday tail. Tie it on him.

PEER. You'll make me look a fool.

OLD MAN. No bare-bum courts my daughter.

PEER. I'm a man, not an animal.

OLD MAN. It's up to you. Wear the tail, court the daughter. You can have an orange bow. Our highest honour.

PEER (*thoughtfully, as before*). 'When in Rome . . .' Tie it on!

OLD MAN. You're learning.

CHAMBERLAIN. Wag it. Give it a wiggle.

PEER (*crossly*). Any more conditions? Renounce Christianity, perhaps?

OLD MAN. No, no. Belief is free. It's outward appearance that makes a troll. Agree with us on style, and believe what you like. So what if it gives us the creeps?

PEER. I could like you. Despite all your conditions. I could like you a lot.

OLD MAN. Son in law, we're not half as black as we're painted – another difference between us and humans. OK, business over. Time to give eyes and ears a treat.
    Music, ho! Let the trollharp sound!
    Dancetrolls, hey! Come tread the ground.

Music. Dancing.

CHAMBERLAIN. What d'you think?

PEER. Er . . .

OLD MAN. Be honest.

PEER. It's awful. A cow on the harp? A sow in ankle socks?

TROLLS. Eat him!

OLD MAN. Human standards. He can't help it.

TROLLWOMEN. Tear his ears off! Gouge his eyes!

WOMAN IN GREEN (*weeping*). Such unkindness! Such insults! When a princess dances and a princess plays.

PEER. Ah. You, was it? Well, you know . . . when a man's having fun. He has his little joke . . .

WOMAN IN GREEN. Swear it was a joke.

PEER. That dancing and playing were . . . something else. Cross my heart.

OLD MAN. Human nature's a funny thing. Hard to get rid of. The more you pick at it, the faster it heals. Look at my son in law. He seemed happy to do anything: chuck off his Christian clothes, drink bull-beer, wear a tail. All I asked. I thought Old Adam was gone for good – but here he is again. It's no good, son in law. You've got chronic human nature. You need the operation.

PEER. What operation?

OLD MAN. Left eyeball. A few scratches, till you see squint. Everything'll look better right away. Better still, when I cut out the other windowpane.

PEER. You're drunk!

The OLD MAN *sets out sharp instruments on a table.*

OLD MAN. My glazier's kit. It's only like blinkering a bull. You'll see your bride in all her beauty. No more harping cows or sows in socks.

PEER. You're out of your mind!

CHAMBERLAIN. His majesty's *in* his mind. You're out.

OLD MAN. Think of the annoyance you won't have anymore. Aren't eyes reservoirs for tears – acid drops?

PEER. 'If thine eye offend thee, pluck it out'. That's in the Bible. But will I ever see again, like now?

OLD MAN. Nevermore.

PEER. Oh well, thanks a lot.

OLD MAN. Now what are you doing?

PEER. Going.

OLD MAN. You can't. Getting in is easy. But the door's one-way. No exit.

PEER. I'm a prisoner?

OLD MAN. Prince Peer, be reasonable. You can be a troll. You've got what it takes. Doesn't he act like a troll already? Don't you want to be one?

PEER. Of course I bloody do. For a wife, wealth, a kingdom, I'll
make sacrifices. But there are limits. I agreed to the tail. But I
can untie it any time. I took off my trousers. But I can slip into
them again whenever I like. I can play the troll – or stop. I can
swear that a cow's a girl, and eat my words. But that other
thing: to know you'll never be free again, you'll be a troll
forever, with no going back, hand to the plough as the Bible
says . . . That makes a man think. I can't do it. Never. No.

OLD MAN. That does it. I don't have to put up with this.
Day-white bastard! Do you know who I am? You play games
with my daughter –

PEER. Liar!

OLD MAN. And now you can marry her.

PEER. What makes you think –

OLD MAN. You fancied her, didn't you? Really fancied her?

PEER (*snorting*). Who bloody cares?

OLD MAN. You humans never change. Always babbling about
your souls, and always on the make. So fancying doesn't
matter? Just you wait. You'll see.

PEER. Now what's your game?

WOMAN IN GREEN. Peer, darling, you're going to be a daddy.

PEER. Unlock the door. I'm going.

OLD MAN. We'll wrap Baby Bunting and send him on.

PEER (*wiping away sweat*). I hate this dream.

OLD MAN. Where shall we send him? Care of the palace?

PEER. Care of the parish.

OLD MAN. Whatever you like, prince Peer. It's up to you. But
remember: what's done is done. Your . . . shoot . . . will grow.
Bastards sprout like weeds.

PEER. Look . . . Old Man . . . calm down. Miss, be reasonable.
Let's talk about it. First, you ought to know: I'm not a prince.
I'm not rich. Weigh me, measure me any way you like. This is
all there is.

The WOMAN IN GREEN *faints.* TROLLSERVANTS *carry her
out. The* OLD MAN *gives* PEER *a long, contemptuous look, then
says:*

OLD MAN. Children, throw him over the cliff.

TROLLCHILDREN. Pa, can't we play with him first? Owls and eagles? Wolves and lambkins? Mouse and cat?

OLD MAN. Yes. Don't be long. I'm cross and tired. Good night!

He goes. The TROLLCHILDREN *begin hunting* PEER.

PEER. Devils! Let me go!

He tries to escape up the chimney.

TROLLCHILDREN. Goblins! Bogles! Bite his bum!

PEER. Ow!

He tries to escape through a trapdoor to the cellar.

TROLLCHILDREN. Stuff every hole!

CHAMBERLAIN. Aren't the children having fun?

PEER *is shaking off a tiny* TROLL, *which has its teeth locked fast in his ear.*

PEER. Let go, you bastard!

CHAMBERLAIN (*rapping his knuckles*). More respect for the prince, you bastard!

PEER. A rathole!

He runs to it.

TROLLCHILDREN. Stuff it, gnomes!

PEER. The old man was foul. The kids are fouler.

TROLLCHILDREN. Skin him!

PEER. Ow! I wish I was a mouse.

The TROLLCHILDREN *swarm all over him.*

TROLLCHILDREN. Get him! Get him!

PEER (*howling*). Yow! I wish I was a louse.

He falls.

TROLLCHILDREN. His eyes!

PEER (*drowning in trolls*). I'm done for! Ma!

Church bells ring in the distance.

TROLLCHILDREN. Bells! Bells! Save us! Aaaahhh!

The TROLLS *scatter in alarm, shrieking. The hall crumbles around them. Everything disappears.*

10.

Pitch darkness. In it, PEER *can be heard, slashing and beating with a treebranch.*

PEER. Answer! Who are you?

VOICE IN THE DARK. Myself.

PEER. Let me pass!

VOICE. Go round, Peer. The mountain's big enough.

PEER tries to pass another way, but his path is blocked.

PEER. Who are you?

VOICE. Myself. Can you say as much?

PEER. I can say what I like. My sword can slash. On guard! Ha! Ho! There! King Saul slew his hundreds, Peer Gynt slew thousands.

He slices wildly about him.

Who are you?

VOICE. Myself.

PEER. Dumb answer. Keep it. It's no good to me. What are you?

VOICE. The Great Bøyg.

PEER. Really? That helps a lot. Bøyg, let me pass.

VOICE. Peer, go round.

PEER. No, through!

He slashes and slices.

He's down!

He tries to pass, but makes no headway.

Ah! Ha! How many are you?

VOICE. The Great Bøyg, Peer. The one and only.
    The Bøyg who was hurt; the Bøyg who's whole;
    The Bøyg who's dead; the Bøyg who lives.

PEER *throws away his branch.*

PEER. My stick's troll-smeared. I'll use my fists.

He hits out wildly.

VOICE. Yes, use your fists. Use all your might.
    Ho, ho, Peer Gynt. You'll win the fight.

PEER (*trying again*). This way, that way, it's all the same. In, out, it's just as far. This side or that side, it's just as narrow. He's here! And here! All round! I punch my way through, and I'm back where I started. Tell me your name. Let me see you. What the Hell are you?

VOICE. The Bøyg.

PEER (*feeling round him*). Not dead. Not alive. Slime. Mist. Shapeless shape. It's like fighting sleepy bears. (*Shouting suddenly.*) Stand and fight!

VOICE. Bøyg's not so dumb.

PEER. Hit me.

VOICE. Bøyg never hits.

PEER. Damn you! Fight!

VOICE. The Great Bøyg wins without a fight.

PEER. I wish goblins were here to fight with. A one-year-old troll. Anything! Not this . . . Now he's snoring. Bøyg!

VOICE. What?

PEER. Use your strength.

VOICE. The Great Bøyg wins by gentleness.

PEER (*biting his own arms and hands*). Claws! Teeth! Gash and tear! Let me see my own blood flow!

We hear the sound of wingbeats from gigantic birds.

BIRD CRIES. Is he near now, Bøyg?

VOICE. Step by step, and foot by foot.

BIRD CRIES. Sisters, hurry! Join the feast!

PEER. If you mean to save me, Solveig, do it now! No time to hang your head and blush. The prayer book! Chuck it in his eye!

BIRD CRIES. He's weakening.

VOICE. He's ours.

BIRD CRIES. Sisters, hurry!

PEER. Life's not worth one hour of this!

He sinks to the ground.

BIRD CRIES. He's down, Bøyg! Take him! Take him!

The VOICE *fades to nothing in a sudden whisper.*

VOICE. He was too strong. His women helped.

11.

Dawn. In the high pastures, outside a hut which belongs to ÅSE. *The door is shut. Everything is empty and still.* PEER *is lying on the ground beside the hut, asleep. He wakes, sits up and gazes round with bleary eyes. He spits.*

PEER. I'd love a pickled herring.

He spits again, and at the same moment sees HELGA *coming in with a foodbasket.*

Hey, young 'un. What brings you here?

HELGA. Solveig said –

PEER (*jumping up*). Where is she?

HELGA. At home.

PEER. Helga . . .

HELGA. If you come any closer, I'll run away.

PEER. D'you know who was here last night? The troll king's daughter, buzzing round me like a horsefly.

HELGA. It was lucky we rang the bells.

PEER. Peer Gynt's too smart for trolls. Eh? What d'you say?

HELGA (*in tears*). Don't touch me!

PEER. Look: here in my pocket. A silver button. It's yours if you
speak up for me.

HELGA. Please let me go.

PEER. Take it, then.

HELGA. Let go. The basket's there!

PEER. God help you if you fail –

HELGA. You're scaring me!

PEER *lets her go.*

PEER (*gently*). It's all right. I just meant . . . ask her not to
forget me.

HELGA *runs away.*

12.

*Deep in a pinewood. Grey autumn day. Snow falling. PEER,
shirt-sleeved, is felling trees. He begins chopping a tall pine with bent
branches.*

PEER. Oh-ya! Be as tough as you like, old man,
    It's a waste of time. You're coming down.
    You think you're safe in your coat of mail.
    But I'll smash that. It won't stop me.

Another blow.

    No use waving your arms. You don't scare me.
    You can huff and puff, yell all you like,
    It'll end just the same: you'll bend the knee.

He stops in sudden disgust.

Who am I kidding? It's not an adversary clad in steel, just an
old fir tree with wrinkled bark. Who am I kidding? It's bad
enough chopping; chopping and daydreaming's just bloody
stupid. Stop, then. No more daydreams. Head out of the
clouds. You're an outlaw. If you leave this wood, you're dead.

He starts chopping again.

An outlaw, right. You've no mother here
To set your table and fetch your food.
If you want to eat, you must help yourself:
Snatch it alive from wood and stream,
Gather sticks and bracken to light a fire,
Fetch and carry, do it all yourself.
Warm clothes, do you want? Go skin a deer.
Build a house? Start breaking the stones,
Start felling the timber, then lug it
Wherever you want it. You're on your own.

He lets the axe drop, as he gazes ahead of him.

I'll build such a beauty! Tower on the roofridge,
Topped with a weather-vane: solid brass.
Carved on the gable, a mermaid,
Girl to the navel, and fish below.
Brass locks and latches. Window glass
That will set strangers wondering
What it is that gleams on the distant hill.

He laughs savagely.

The hell with daydreams! You're an outlaw.

He starts chopping fiercely.

You need a bark-thatched hut, to keep out frost and rain.
Nothing else.

He looks up at the tree.

He's leaning. He's weakening.
One more blow, and he'll measure his length,
Making the undergrowth shudder and shake.

He starts lopping the branches. Then he stops, and stands listening, with upraised axe.

Someone's there! It's Ingrid's Pa!
The old man from Haegstad, creeping up on me.

He ducks behind the tree, and looks out.

A lad. Just one. Looks scared to death.
Glancing about. What's he hiding
Under his jacket? A sickle. He's stopped.
Looks round. Spreads out his hand,
Flat on a treestump. Braces himself.

What now? Ah! Not his finger!
Chopped off his own finger. He's bleeding
Like a stuck pig. He's wrapped up his hand
In a cloth. Now he's running away.

He gets up.

Bloody fool! You can't just . . . a finger!
Clean off – no accident. Ha! Now I get it.
The call-up. Serving his majesty. Not any more.
Even so . . . your own finger. Forever.
I might have *thought* of that. Planned it.
Intended. But done it? No chance!

He shakes his head, and goes back to work.

13.

Room in ÅSE's *house. Chaos. The chest is open, and clothes are
scattered everywhere. A cat in the bed.* ÅSE *and her neighbour* KARI *are
frantically collecting things together and putting them in order.* ÅSE
runs to one side.

ÅSE. Listen, Kari –

KARI. What?

   ÅSE runs to the other side.

ÅSE. Listen . . . where did I . . . have you seen . . . what am I
looking for? I'm going crazy. Where's the chest key?

KARI. In the keyhole.

ÅSE. What's that rumbling?

KARI. The last cartload going to Haegstad.

ÅSE (*weeping*). I wish it was me in my coffin. God help me! The
whole house emptied to pay the fine. What him at Haegstad
left, the bailiff took. I've hardly the clothes I stand up in!
Shame on them! How could they ask such a fine?

She sits on the edge of the bed.

The farm's gone . . . the land . . . our whole inheritance. The
old man was tough, but the judge was far tougher. No one to
pity me. No one to turn to. Peer far away.

KARI. They left you this house, till the day you die.

ÅSE. Charity!

KARI. God help you, Åse. Peer's cost you dear.

ÅSE. Peer? You're off your head! Ingrid came back safe and sound, didn't she? It's the Devil they should blame. It's all his fault. The bastard tempted my poor boy.

KARI. Shall I fetch the parson? Things may be worse than you think.

ÅSE. Yes. Why not?

She gets up.

I can't! I'm his mother. I must help him. I'm all he's got. Look, they left this coat. I'll patch it. If only I'd dared to keep the bedcover! Where are those socks?

KARI. There, in that pile of rags.

ÅSE (*rummaging*). Look, Kari. The old casting-ladle. He used to play at making buttons. Melting, shaping, stamping. Once, when there were people here, he came in and asked his pa for a bit of tin. 'Not tin,' says Jon, 'His majesty's good coin. Solid silver – you're Jon Gynt's son.' God forgive him, drunk as a lord. Silver, tin, it was all the same to him. Here are the socks. Full of holes. I'll darn them, Kari. Then I'll lie down. I'm worn out. (*Excitedly.*) Look! A flannel shirt! They missed it. We can surely keep it. The one he's got is so thin and worn.

KARI. It's stealing, Åse. It's a sin.

ÅSE. God forgives our sins. That's what parson says.

14.

In the forest, outside a newly built hut. Reindeer horns over the door. Deep snow. Nightfall. PEER is standing outside the door, hammering a heavy wooden bolt in place. As he works, he chuckles to himself.

PEER. Fasten the bolt and bolt the door.
    Bolt out the trolls, bolt out the people.
    Fasten the bolt and bolt the door.
    Bolt out the goblins, swarming like midges,

Hammering, tapping. 'Peer, open up!
Welcome us! Quicksilver, thought-fast,
Darting and rummaging, under the bed,
Sparks in the chimney, scatter of ash.
Hee hee! Peer, do you really expect
Nails and planks to bolt out goblin-thoughts?'

SOLVEIG, *with a shawl over her head and a bundle in her hand,*
skis down over the fellside.

SOLVEIG. God bless your work. Don't send me away. You asked
me to come.

PEER. Solveig! You're not afraid?

SOLVEIG. You sent Helga with a message. Wind and silence
brought more messages. Your mother's stories, my dreams,
dull nights and empty days, all told me 'Go to him!' Down
there my life was smothered. I couldn't laugh or cry. I'd no
idea what you were thinking. I just knew that I must, I had to.

PEER. But your father? -

SOLVEIG. In God's wide world, I've no Father or Mother now.
I've left them forever.

PEER. Solveig – for me?

SOLVEIG. For you alone. You must be everything to me: friend,
comforter . . . (*In tears.*) The worst was leaving Helga . . .
leaving father . . . leaving mother who cradled me. God
forgive me, the worst was leaving all of them.

PEER. You know the judgement passed last spring? They've
taken my farm, my inheritance.

SOLVEIG. It wasn't your inheritance that tore me from all I
loved.

PEER. You know the rest of it? If I step outside this forest, I'm
anyone's. Fair game.

SOLVEIG. I came on skis. I asked the way. 'Where to?' they
asked. I answered, 'Home'.

PEER. Who needs nails and planks? Who needs bolts against
goblin-thoughts? If you go inside, if you make it home, you
bless it against all evil. Solveig, let me look at you. You're so
bright, so pure! Let me lift you. How slim, how light you are! I
could carry you forever, darling, and never tire. You're so

warm, so pretty. Who'd have thought I could ever make you love me? The thing I longed for, day and night. Look, this is the house I've built. It's too small. A hut. I'll pull it down.

SOLVEIG. Hut or palace, I'm happy here. I can breathe; the air is pure. It was smothering down there. But here, where the wind sighs in the trees. Stillness and song! This is my home.

PEER. Forever?

SOLVEIG. There's no going back.

PEER. Go in. Let me see you in the house. I'll gather sticks, light a fire. You'll sit there softly, and never be cold.

He unlocks the door, and SOLVEIG *goes in. He stands silent for a moment, then laughs and jumps for joy.*

My princess! At last she's found!
Palace! Grow here, on this ground!

He takes his axe and goes towards the trees. An old WOMAN *in a tattered green dress comes from the wood. An ugly* CHILD *limps beside her, clutching her skirt in one hand and a beer bottle in the other.*

WOMAN. Good evening, Quickfoot.

PEER. Who the hell are you?

WOMAN. Old friends, Peer Gynt. Neighbours. We live just over there.

PEER. News to me.

WOMAN. You built your hut; I built mine.

PEER (*moving away*). I'm in a rush . . .

WOMAN. You always were. But I still caught up with you.

PEER. You've got the wrong man.

WOMAN. I got the wrong man years ago. When you made those promises.

PEER. Promises? What the hell – ?

WOMAN. Have you forgotten that night at my father's? When you drank that . . . ? Have you forgotten?

PEER. How can I forget what I never knew? What are you talking about? When did we last meet?

WOMAN. The last time was the first time. (*To the* CHILD.) Give your Pa a drink. He's thirsty.

PEER. Pa? You're drunk. I – you – he – ?

WOMAN. I can tell an onion by its skin. See for yourself. He's lame in his legs; you're lame in your brain.

PEER. You're joking.

WOMAN. You're wriggling.

PEER. That beanpole?

WOMAN. He sprouted fast.

PEER. You – a wrinkled old troll – and me . . .

WOMAN. Bastard! (*Weeping.*) I can't help it if I'm not as beautiful as I was then, when you tricked me on the mountain. He was born in autumn. There was only the Devil for midwife. If you want me like I was before, chuck out that girl in there. Out of sight, out of mind. Do that, dear sweet Peer, and see how pretty I can be.

PEER. Witch! Get out of here.

WOMAN. I won't.

PEER. I'll make you.

WOMAN. Try. I'll be here every day, peering round the door, watching. You'll be sitting together, the pair of you. You feel like a kiss, a cuddle – and there I'll be, demanding my share. Her turn, then mine. Dear sweet Peer. Marry her tomorrow. I'll see you then.

PEER. Bitch!

WOMAN. I nearly forgot. Little Quickfoot. You have to foster him. Go on, bratlegs. Run to Pa.

The CHILD *spits at* PEER.

CHILD. I'll chop your head off. Wait and see.

WOMAN (*kissing him*). That's a good boy. When you grow up, you'll be just like your Pa.

PEER (*stamping his foot*). To hell with the pair of you!

WOMAN. We're here, and here we stay.

PEER (*clenching his fists*). And all this comes –

WOMAN. – from fancying! Well hard luck, Peer.

PEER. Harder luck for her, my pure, my darling Solveig.

WOMAN. As the Devil said when his Ma thrashed him because his Pa got drunk, 'It's the pure what gets the blame.'

She goes into the forest with the CHILD, *who tosses the bottle away behind him.* PEER *stands a long time without speaking.*

PEER. 'Go round,' said the Bøyg. It's the only way.
    My palace has crashed down round my ears.
    I was so near to Solveig, and now there's a wall.
    Everything's spoiled. Joy was yesterday.
    Go round, Peer. There's no way through,
    No passage direct from you to her.
    Wait! There may be. There may be a way.
    Repentance, the Bible says. Something like . . .
    No, I've forgotten. I haven't a Bible.
    Here in this wild wood, there's no one to help.

    Repentance? It might take me years.
    Years of misery, tearing apart
    All that's decent and holy and fair,
    Then cobbling it back again, piece by piece.
    It's easy to fix an old fiddle – but who
    Knows how to patch up a broken bell?
    Who treads on green shoots and expects them to grow?

    I'll go round. I'll find a way. Long or short,
    I'll find a way . . .

SOLVEIG (*at the door*). Are you coming?

PEER (*under his breath*). Go round.

SOLVEIG. What?

PEER. You must wait. It's dark. I've a heavy load.

SOLVEIG. I'll help you. We'll carry it together.

PEER. No. Stay there. I'll carry it.

SOLVEIG. Don't be long.

PEER. Be patient. Long or short, please wait.

SOLVEIG (*nodding to him*). I'll wait.

PEER *goes out, along the forest path.* SOLVEIG *stands in the open half-door, looking after him.*

15.

ÅSE'*s hut. Evening. A wood fire burns on the hearth, lighting the room. A cat on a chair at the foot of the bed.* ÅSE *is lying in the bed, restlessly plucking at the cover.*

ÅSE. O God, will he never come? The hours pass so slowly. I've so much to tell him. No time to waste. So soon! Who'd have thought it? If I'd known, I'd have been so much kinder.

    PEER *comes in.*

PEER. Hello, Ma.

ÅSE. Peer! Thank God! But how did you dare to come? If they find you, they'll kill you.

PEER. Never mind. I had to come now.

ÅSE. Kari was wrong. Now I can go in peace.

PEER. What d'you mean? Go where?

ÅSE. It'll soon be over. Not long to wait.

    PEER *turns away and walks across the room.*

PEER. I ran from misery. I thought here was safe. Are you cold? Your feet? Your hands?

ÅSE. Yes, Peer. Not long now. When my eyes mist over, close them gently. Then get me a coffin – a good one. No, I forgot . . .

PEER. Hush, Ma. Don't talk about that now.

ÅSE. Yes, yes.

    She looks uneasily round the hut.

    Who else cares? Look how little they've left.

PEER (*wincing*). Again! (*Harshly.*) I know it's my fault. But why not let it rest?

ÅSE. It wasn't you. It was that bloody drink. You were drunk, darling. You didn't mean it. Then there was that reindeer ride. No wonder you felt peculiar.

PEER. That nonsense! Forget it. Forget the whole thing. Don't be sad. Let's be sad another day.

He sits on the side of the bed.

Change the subject, Ma. Let's have a gossip. Nothing serious or sad. What's new in the village?

ÅSE (*smiling*). They say there's a girl here pines for the mountains.

PEER (*quickly*). Mads Moen. How's he these days?

ÅSE. They say her Ma and Pa can cry all they like, she won't listen. You talk to her, Peer. You know what to say.

PEER. Aslak. How's Aslak?

ÅSE. Never mind Aslak! That pig. Let me tell you that little girl's name . . .

PEER. Change the subject, Ma. Nothing serious or sad. D'you want a drink? Have you room in that bed? It's tiny. Look! It's mine. When I was a boy. D'you remember how you sat here every evening, smoothing the covers, singing nursery rhymes?

ÅSE. D'you remember playing sleighrides? Your Pa was away. The covers were sleigh-rugs. The floor was an icy fjord.

PEER. And the best bit – d'you remember? The fiery steeds!

ÅSE. We borrowed Kari's cat. Sat him on a stool.

PEER. West of the moon, east of the sun, to Soria-Moria Castle! That stick from the cupboard, our sleigh-whip!

ÅSE. I was the driver. I sat in front.

PEER. You shook the reins, and kept turning round as we galloped, to ask if I was cold. God bless you, dear old Ma. What a silly old soul you were. What's the matter? You're groaning.

ÅSE. This bed's so hard.

PEER. Sit up. I'll hold you. There.

ÅSE (*restless*). Peer, I'm ready.

PEER. Ready for what?

ÅSE. It's all I want.

PEER. Don't be daft. Pull the blanket round. Let me sit on the bed. That's it. Now, d'you remember those nursery rhymes?

ÅSE. Give me my prayerbook. I've so much to think about.

PEER. In Soria-Moria castle, they're giving a banquet. The king, the prince. Lie back in the sleigh, Ma. I'll have you there in a moment.

ÅSE. Peer, dear, am I invited?

PEER. We both are.

He throws a cord round the chair with the cat on it, takes a stick in his hand and sits on the foot of the bed.

Hup! Faster, there, Blackie! Ma, you're not cold? Aha! Grane's galloping, kicking his heels.

ÅSE. What's that ringing?

PEER. Sleighbells, Ma.

ÅSE. So deep and muffled.

PEER. We're crossing the fjord.

ÅSE. I'm frightened. It's roaring, it's sighing.

PEER. Wind in the fir-trees. Be still, Ma.

ÅSE. Lights in the distance, winking and glowing. Where are they, Peer?

PEER. In the windows and doors of the castle. Can you hear dancing?

ÅSE. Yes.

PEER. Saint Peter's at the gate. 'Come in,' he'll say.

ÅSE. Will he kiss my hand?

PEER. With reverence. He'll offer you sweet wine.

ÅSE. And cake?

PEER. Platefuls! And the parson's wife'll bring coffee and biscuits.

ÅSE. Will she say hello?

PEER. As often as you like.

ÅSE. What a wonderful party you're driving me to.

PEER (*cracking the whip*). Hup! Gee up there, Blackie!

ÅSE. Darling Peer. This is the right road?

PEER (*cracking the whip again*). Wide and clear.

ÅSE. I feel so tired . . .

PEER. There's the castle, just down the road. Not much further.

ÅSE. I'll lie back. I'll shut my eyes. Darling Peer, I'll leave it all to you.

PEER. Gee up there, Grane! Fast as you can.
    The castle is crowded. The guests
    Flock to the windows. 'They're coming!
    Peer Gynt and his mother are here!'
    Beg pardon, Saint Peter? 'Keep out!'?
    There's no honester, worthier soul.
    Don't fret about me. I'll stay here.
    Take me or leave me, I'm not fussed.
    Like Satan himself in the pulpit,
    I've told such a packet of lies.
    I called her a cackling old hen,
    Always scolding and nagging –
    But that's not for you. Show respect,
    And make her feel really at home.
    The salt of the earth! Her ladyship!
    Hoho! God the father in person!
    You're for it now, Peter! You'll catch it!

In a deep voice.

    'Who told you to play high and mighty?
    She's welcome. Let Åse come in!'

He laughs loudly and turns to her.

Didn't I tell you? That's changed his tune. (*Anxiously.*) Why are you looking so pop-eyed? Ma? Don't be daft, Ma.

He goes to the head of the bed.

Stop staring. Say something. It's me. It's Peer.

Cautiously, he feels her forehead and hands. Then he throws the cord down on the chair and says quietly:

Whoa, Grane. Journey's end.

He closes her eyes and bends over her.

Thanks for everything, Ma. Slaps, night-night kisses, everything. Now you thank me.

He brushes his cheek against her lips.

What was that? 'Good night, sleep tight'?

KARI *comes in.*

KARI. Peer? She'll be so glad to see you! Her prayers are answered. How fast asleep she is. Dear God, she's not – ?

PEER. Shhh! She's dead.

KARI weeps by ÅSE's body. PEER walks up and down the room. Finally he goes to stand by the bed.

PEER. See that she's decently buried. I have to go.

KARI. Will you go far?

PEER. To the sea-coast.

KARI. So far?

PEER. Even further.

He goes.

End of Part One

PART TWO

16.

*Grove of palms on the south west coast of Morocco. A laden table stands
on rush matting under a parasol. In the background, hammocks hang
from the branches. A steamyacht is anchored in the bay, flying the
Norwegian and US flags. A dinghy is drawn up on the shore.* PEER, *a
handsome, middle-aged man in elegant travelling clothes, with gold
pince-nez hanging on his chest, is entertaining* COTTON, BALLON,
EBERKOPF *and* TRUMPETBLAST. *They have finished their meal,
and* PEER *is pouring wine.*

PEER. Drink up, gentlemen! If the gods insist that we enjoy
   ourselves, let's make the best of it. Here we are in Morocco
   . . . glorious afternoon . . . palms . . . a feast before us . . . and
   there in the bay my yacht waits to carry us who knows where?
   Chance threw us together, gentlemen. We're travelling
   companions, enjoying each other's company as we discover
   the world. Drink up!

TRUMPETBLAST. Friend Gynt, you're the perfect host.

PEER. No no. Some credit goes to my bank manager, my cook,
   my steward.

COTTON. OK, OK. We'll drink to them as well.

BALLON. But it's you, Monsieur, who has the *gout*, the *ton*, the
   – how shall I put it – ?

EBERKOPF. Interiority . . . manofthewholewideworldliness . . .
   quintessence of *Ur-natur*. Is that what you mean, Monsieur?

BALLON. It has a different ring in French.

EBERKOPF. Such a cramped tongue! But if we ask the cause of
   this phenomenon –

PEER. Simple, gentlemen. It's because I never married. To
   yourself be true. That's my philosophy. Look out for Number
   One. You can't do that if you're a pack-camel for someone
   else's wellbeing.

EBERKOPF. This to-oneself-betrueness was not won without struggle?

PEER. When I was younger, yes. There was one occasion . . . I was almost caught. I was a handsome sprig of a lad. She was a princess.

COTTON. Ha! That was the end of that.

BALLON. Her family disapproved?

PEER. Quite the opposite! There were reasons . . . you understand . . . not to put the wedding off. But the whole thing was wrong for me from first to last. I'm particular. My own master. So when her father began hinting that I should change my name, give up my titles – and other conditions, even less palatable – I pulled straight out of it. Refused the father's terms, turned the daughter down.

BALLON. Was that the end of it?

PEER. By no means. There was quite a to-do. At one point I was fighting seven of her young relatives. A bloody business, even if I did win through. One thing it does show: there's a destiny that shapes our ends.

EBERKOPF. Such a philosopher you are! And yet, you say, you never went to school?

PEER. Self-taught, entirely. (*He lights a cigar. Throughout what follows, he stealthily fills and refills his glass.*) But gentlemen, just look at my career. What had I when I first came West? Empty hands. But Luck was on my side. I did well – and the more careful I was, the more I prospered. Ten years on, people began calling me the Croesus of the Charlestown traders. My reputation travelled from port to port. Every cargo brought success.

COTTON. What was your cargo?

PEER. Heathen idols, mainly, bound for China. I know what you're going to say. An immoral trade. I agree. I found it odious. I'm always alert to what they call 'cause and effect'. If I overstep the bounds, I worry. Also, I wasn't getting any younger. Nearly fifty, a few grey hairs. I've a perfect constitution, but doubts still nagged. 'Who knows how long there is left? How long till the Great Assizes, the separation of sheep and goats?' It was a problem. Stop the Chinese trade?

Impossible. Then I hit on a solution. A second trade, also to China. In spring: idols. In autumn: missionaries, with everything needed for converting people: Bibles, stockings, rum, rice –

COTTON. All at a profit?

PEER. Naturally. It was a huge success. For every idol sold, one coolie was baptized. It cancelled out exactly. My missionaries were working day and night, counteracting the inflow of idols.

EBERKOPF (*clinking glasses with him*). Such a lifeplan stirs the blood. So theory-free! So practical!

PEER. We Northerners know how to plan campaigns. The secret of success is simple: tread fearlessly, avoid life's pitfalls, look to the horizon – and always keep a bridge behind to fall back on. That's my theory, learned at my mother's knee.

BALLON. You're Norwegian, aren't you?

PEER. By birth, yes. But by inclination, a citizen of the world. For all my financial success, I have to thank America. For my well-stocked library, I'm grateful to Germany. France gave me my style in clothes, my *savoir faire.* England taught me to work hard – especially for myself. From Italy, a smattering of *dolce far niente* – and once or twice, in a really tight spot, I fought my way clear with the help of Swedish steel.

TRUMPETBLAST (*lifting his glass*). Swedish steel.

EBERKOPF. We'll drink to that!

They clink glasses and drink with PEER. *He is clearly tipsy.*

COTTON. You're a fine man, sir, and that's a fine speech. But now, this wealth of yours: how d'you mean to use it?

PEER (*smiling*). Aha! Use it? First: to travel. That's why I invited you to join me. In Gibraltar. Company. A chorus to dance round my golden calf.

EBERKOPF. So witty!

COTTON. But you've more in mind than travelling. Another goal. A life's ambition –

PEER. To be Emperor.

THE OTHERS. What? Where?

PEER. Emperor of the world.

BALLON. My friend, but how?

PEER. By the power of gold. It's not a new plan, by any means.
It's behind everything I've done. When I was a boy, I soared in
a cloud-chariot across the sea, in dreams. I've never wavered.
It says somewhere, 'Win all the world, but to yourself be true,
or count your glory but a wreath on an empty skull'.
Something like that. That's not just words. It's true.

EBERKOPF. Be true to yourself. But what is the Gyntish self?

PEER. The world in here, inside my noddle. That's what makes
me *me* and no one else – unless God's the Devil in disguise.

TRUMPETBLAST. I understand.

BALLON. Such vision!

EBERKOPF. Such poetry!

PEER (*carried away*). The Gyntish self! An army of wishes,
appetites, desires! The Gyntish self! A sea of fancies, claims,
demands. My heartbeat! My breath of life! But just as the
Good Lord needed common clay to make the world, so, if I'm
to be Emperor, I must have gold.

BALLON. You've got gold.

PEER. Not enough! That's why we set sail tonight. North.
There's a newspaper on board, with important news.

He gets up and lifts his glass.

Fortune helps those who help themselves.

THE OTHERS. What news?

PEER. Hellas has risen.

THE OTHERS (*jumping up*). What? The Greeks –

PEER. – are revolting. And Turkey's on the ropes!

He drains his glass.

BALLON. The gate to glory opens! Weapons from France –

EBERKOPF. Discreet support.

COTTON. If the price is right.

BALLON (*embracing* PEER). *Mon ami*, forgive me. I misjudged
you.

EBERKOPF (*shaking his hand*). Such a fool I was. I took you for a crook.

COTTON. Oh, not that. Maybe an idiot . . .

TRUMPETBLAST (*trying to kiss him*). Cousin Gynt, we were all mistaken.

PEER. What d'you mean?

EBERKOPF. The Gyntish army. Wishes, appetites, desires!

BALLON (*with great respect*). Monsieur, we understand.

PEER. What's going on?

BALLON. You don't know?

PEER. Damned if I do.

BALLON. You mean, you *aren't* going to take your ship and your money and help the Greeks?

PEER (*snorting*). No thanks! I back winners. I'll help the Turks.

BALLON. *Incroyable!*

EBERKOPF. So witty!

PEER *pauses, then leans on a chair and says seriously:*

PEER. Gentlemen, it's time we parted, before the rags of our friendship blow away like smoke. A man with nothing can risk all he has. But someone who's made his pile, like me, has more to lose. *You* go to Greece. I'll provide all the weapons you want for them. Free. The more you fan the war, the more I stand to gain. Make it hot for Turkey, end your days in glory, spiked on a spearpoint. But count me out. (*Slapping his pockets.*) I've money, and I have Sir Peter Gynt – myself!

He puts up his parasol and goes to the edge of the grove where the hammocks are swinging.

TRUMPETBLAST. The bastard.

BALLON. No honour.

COTTON. Forget honour. Think of the money!

He shakes his fist at the yacht.

Think of that booby's gold, locked on that ship of his.

EBERKOPF. You inspire me. Come! At once. His empire is doomed. Hurrah!

BALLON. What d'you mean?

EBERKOPF. Mutiny! We bribe the crew. I take over the yacht –

COTTON. You what?

EBERKOPF. I grab the lot.

He goes to the dinghy.

COTTON. I'm grabbing with you.

He goes after him.

TRUMPETBLAST. What a bounder!

BALLON. No honour. But . . . *enfin* . . .

He hurries after them.

TRUMPETBLAST. I'll tag along. But under protest. Wait!

He, too, goes.

17.

Another part of the coast. Moonlight, scudding clouds. The yacht is heading full speed out to sea. PEER *runs along the shore, pinching himself, staring out to sea.*

PEER. It's a nightmare! I'm dreaming! I've got to wake up!
    They're sailing away from here. Full speed ahead.
    I'm dreaming. I'm seeing things. I'm out of my mind.

He wrings his hands.

    I'm done for. Not likely. I'm not going to die.

He tears his hair.

    I'm dreaming. Please let me be dreaming. God, please!
    It's a scandal; it's true, though. I trusted them too!
    Lord God, are you listening? Justice and truth!

He stretches up his arms.

    It's me. Peter Gynt. Can you see me? Down here!
    Take care of me, Lord, or you may see me die.
    Please slacken their speed. Make them lower the boat.
    Arrest them. Make something go wrong with the works.

Do listen. Ignore other people. Help *me*!
The world can look after itself for five minutes.
No. He's not listening. He's deaf as a post.
That's brilliant! Our father. God. Stuck for ideas!

He gestures at the sky.

Look, surely . . . I sent all those missions to China.
I mean, one good turn . . . Can't you get me on board?

A sudden glare of light from the yacht fills the sky. Thick smoke pours out. There is a loud explosion. PEER *shrieks and throws himself on the sand. The smoke gradually clears, and when it has gone, so has the yacht.* PEER *is pale and quiet.*

A judgement. Paf! Sunk with all hands. Thank you God,
For listening and helping, ignoring my faults!

He breathes out: a long, slow breath.

Ah! Private protection! Yes, now I feel safe!
What, here in this desert? No water? No food?
Don't worry. The Lord understands.

In a loud, ingratiating voice.

                                He'll not suffer
This poor little sparrow to perish. Be humble.
Don't pester. Don't panic. The Lord will provide.

He jumps up, terrified.

A lion! In the bullrushes. Roaring. I heard it!

With chattering teeth.

What nonsense!

Pulling himself together.

                No, really? You heard it? A lion?
I think, all the same, I'll just look for a tree.

He climbs a tree, and settles himself comfortably.

Delightful to feel so uplifted! To stretch
One's soul! So much better than piling up riches!
Put your trust in the Lord. He knows just how deep
In the cup of affliction a person can drink.
He takes such a fatherly interest. He cares.

He casts an eye over the sea, and whispers with a sigh:

Economical, though – ha! Not a chance!

18.

Night. Moroccan camp on the edge of the desert. SOLDIERS *resting round a watchfire. A* SLAVE *runs in, tearing his hair.*

SLAVE. His majesty's charger has vanished!

A SECOND SLAVE *runs in, rending his garments.*

SECOND SLAVE. His majesty's clothes have gone missing!

The OFFICER *hurries in.*

OFFICER. A hundred lashes each, unless they're found!

The WARRIORS *leap on their horses and gallop off in all directions.*

19.

Dawn in the clump of acacias and palms. PEER *is up a tree, using a broken-off branch to fight off a swarm of apes.*

PEER. What a night! Monkeys. Bloody monkeys. What d'you want? God damn it, this is *my* tree. Go away.

Lays about him with the branch.

Bastards! What's that they're throwing? Fruit. Oh. Not fruit. Christ, apes are disgusting. All I wanted was a quiet night. Here they are again! Go on, wah! Shoo! Who's that up there? An old one, with his arms full of . . .

He crouches down and stays still for a moment. Then he tries coaxing.

Here, boy. Good boy. There's a good boy. You're not going to throw that, are you? I'm your friend. Ai ai, oo oo. See, I speak your language. Good boy. Aaargh! The whole armful. Christ, here come the little ones!

Slashing and stabbing with the branch.

Get out of it! Ugh! The father was foul, but the children are fouler!

20.

Early morning. Rocky outcrop overlooking the desert. On one side: rock wall with a cave. Two THIEVES *are standing there. They have the stolen clothes and horse. The horse is tied to a rock. Sound of horsemen in the distance. N.B. In the original, the* THIEVES' *dialogue was recitative, meant to be sung or spoken rhythmically over music.*

FIRST THIEF. Spearblades glimmering,
    Swordtips shimmering,
    Wow! Wow!

SECOND THIEF. Axeblade chopping,
    Headbone hopping,
    Ow! Ow!

The FIRST THIEF *strikes a pose, folding his arms.*

FIRST THIEF. Daddy was a bandit,
    Big and bad.

SECOND THIEF. I'll be a bandit,
    Just like dad.

THIEVES. To yourself be true!
    Be true to you!

The FIRST THIEF *listens.*

FIRST THIEF. Footsteps! Humming!
    Someone's coming!
    No! No!

SECOND THIEF. Don't stand gaping.
    Try escaping.
    Go! Go!

They run for it, leaving their spoils. Noise of the horsemen disappearing in the distance. PEER *comes in, cutting a reed pipe. N.B. In the original production, this was the moment when Grieg's piece 'Morning', a limpid flute solo, was played.*

PEER. What a beautiful morning! Dung-beetles, trundling their loads. Snails, opening their windows.

He puts on his pince-nez.

A toad. In a lump of sandstone. Only his head visible. Watching the world go by. True to himself. (*Thoughtfully.*)

True to himself? Where have I heard that before? It's no good. The older I grow, the worse my memory.

He sits down in the shade.

It's cool here. I'll rest my feet.

He lights a cigar, stretches and gazes out across the desert.

What a boundless expanse. That's an ostrich over there. What on Earth was God thinking of, to make such a wilderness? Is that the sea, glittering in the east? A mirage. The sea's in the west. Dammed from the desert by sand-dunes.

A thought strikes him.

> Dammed. Just a minute! Those dunes are low.
> Dammed. So a cutting . . . a short canal . . .
> Lifegiving water, flooding the sand,
> Turning the desert to cool, clear sea.
> Islands instead of oases. Pasture.
> Sailing-boats skimming like birds where once
> Camel-trains plodded their weary way.
> Green grass fringing the swaying palms.
> In an oasis, lapped by the sea,
> Norsemen will settle, the royal race –
> And there, in a bay with a sloping shore,
> Peeropolis, my royal capital.
> Time to retire, old world! Time to give way
> To Gyntiana, my new found land!

He jumps to his feet.

Cash in hand, that's all I need. My kingdom – well, half my kingdom – for a horse!

The horse neighs in the ravine.

A horse! Clothes . . . jewels . . . weapons.

He goes closer.

They say faith moves mountains. But *horses?*

He puts on the clothes and admires himself.

Sir Peter. A Mahdi from tip to toe. One just never knows. Here, Grane. Steady, boy!

He climbs into the saddle.

Gold stirrups. You can tell a prince by the steed he rides!

He gallops off into the desert.

21.

Sheikh's tent, standing by itself in an oasis. PEER, *in his Muslim clothes, is taking his ease on cushions, drinking coffee and smoking a hookah.* ANITRA *and a troupe of* GIRLS *are dancing and singing for him.*

GIRLS. The Lord has come.
    The holy one.
    Sound flute! Sound drum!
    The Lord has come.

ANITRA. His charger white as the milk that flows
    In the rivers of Paradise above.
    Bend every knee! Bow low!
    His eye bright as the star that glows
    In the velvet sky, alight with love.
    Bend every knee! Bow low!
    Before him, light. Behind him, night.
    Drought, out! No room for the dread Simoom.

GIRLS. Sound flute! Sound drum!
    The Lord has come.

The GIRLS *dance to soft music.*

PEER. Nothing in Charlestown ever equalled this. These Mahdis have got it made. No pretending: just be yourself.

ANITRA *approaches the entrance.*

ANITRA. Master...

PEER. What is it, slave?

ANITRA. They're waiting outside. The sons of the desert. Craving a glimpse of your glory.

PEER. No chance. They can stay where they are. No *man* enters the presence. My children, dance! Your Master's heart is heavy. Lighten it!

The GIRLS *dance.* PEER *has his eye on* ANITRA.

What a beauty! True, her feet could be cleaner. But that's no
discouragement. Quite the reverse, in fact. Anitra, hey!

ANITRA (*coming closer*). As Master commands.

PEER. Delightful child! Your Master is . . . moved. I'll prove it.
I'll make you a houri in Paradise.

ANITRA. Impossible, master. I haven't a soul.

PEER. Leave that to me. I'll see to it. It's true you're stupid. But
you've room inside for soul. Come here. Let me measure your
brainpan. I was right, there's room. There's room.

ANITRA. Master is kind –

PEER. What is it? Speak!

ANITRA. If Master pleases, I'm not really bothered about a soul.
I'd rather have –

PEER. What?

ANITRA (*pointing to his turban*). That pretty opal.

Enraptured, PEER *hands her the jewel.*

PEER. Anitra, what a girl you are! A lass unparalleled, as
someone said.

22.

Moonlight. Grove of trees outside ANITRA*'s tent.* PEER *is sitting
under a tree, holding an Arab lute. His hair and beard are trimmed; he
looks much younger. He plays and sings. N.B. The Norwegian words
are doggerel, too.*

PEER. I locked the gate of Paradise
      And took away the key.
      Far, far I sailed from northern skies,
      While lovely women filled their eyes
      And wept beside the sea.

      South, ever south my voyage lay,
      Salt sea-waves butting past.
      Until, where palmtrees nod and sway
      Like garlands round the ocean bay,
      I burned my boat at last.

I climbed on board a desert ship,
With legs – one, two, three, four.
It sped along. I cracked the whip.
A bird of passage! See me skip!
I flutter, swoop and soar.

Anitra, sweet as sweet palm wine.
Believe me, sweet, it's true.
On goat's milk cheese I love to dine,
But goat's milk cheese is not so fine,
Anitra sweet, as you.

He slings the lute over his shoulder and goes closer to the tent. He speaks.

Silence. Was my sweetheart listening? Did she hear my little song? Is she playing hide and seek inside, peeping out with nothing on? Shh! A cork from a bottle? Again. Someone sighing for love? No, snoring. Sweet music. Anitra sleeps. Nightingales, lay off clucking and gurgling. What bliss, to listen while my darling sleeps . . . To lift the cup . . . to touch it to the lips . . . She's coming. That's even better.

ANITRA (*from inside the tent*). Master? Did you call?

PEER. Sweet child!

He sits under a tree and pulls her to him.

Come here! Let's sit where the palmtree waves.

ANITRA (*lying at his feet*). Your words are sweet music. Even when I don't understand them. Master, tell me, if your servant just listens, can she get a soul?

PEER. A soul shall be yours presently, my girl: the light of life. When Dawn's rosy fingers streak the sky, will be time enough to start your education. Now, in the stillness of night, if I started playing the schoolmaster, raking together wellworn worldly wisdom, I'd be an idiot. In any case, when you come down to it, hearts matter more than souls.

ANITRA. Master, say on! Your words to me are as the gleam of opals.

PEER. To be clever is daft. Where cowardice buds, cruelty blossoms. D'you know what life is?

ANITRA. Please teach me.

PEER. Life is walking dryfooted down the stream of time. Youth! I plan to lord it like a sultan, proud and strong. Not in Gyntiana's palms and pines. In the lush green pastures of a young girl's heart. That's why your empty little noddle's such a blessing. If someone has a soul, self's all they think about. Instead of soul, take me – far better for us both. Look, to settle it, here's an anklet. Let me fasten it...

ANITRA *snores*.

Asleep? Did she miss everything I said? No. It shows my power. My torrent of sweet nothings carried her off to the land of dreams.

He gets up and lays jewels in her lap.

Here are jewels! Anitra, sleep – and dream of Peer. In dreams you crown your kaiser. First prize for personality – that's what Peer Gynt wins tonight!

23.

Caravan route. Just visible in the distance, the oasis. PEER, *on his white horse, is galloping through the desert, with* ANITRA *in front of him on the saddle-bow.*

ANITRA. Stop! I'll bite!

PEER. You minx!

ANITRA. What is it you want?

PEER. To play hawk and dove. To carry you off. To be irresponsible.

ANITRA. For shame! An old man! A Mahdi!

PEER. Not so much of the old. Does this seem old to you?

He tries to kiss her.

Hey! No pecking. What a sharp little bird it is!

ANITRA. Give me that ring on your finger.

PEER. Take it, darling. Take them all!

ANITRA. Your words are sweet music.

PEER. What bliss to be loved like this! I'll dismount. I'll lead the horse. I'll be your slave.

He hands her the whip and dismounts.

There now, my rose, my loveliest flower. I'll tramp through the sand, till I faint from sunstroke and have to stop. I'm young, Anitra, remember that!

ANITRA. Young, yes. Have you other rings?

PEER. I'm young! Here, take these. Like a reindeer, I prance and dance. If I had vineleaves, I'd bind them in my hair. My soul is young. I'm dancing! See me dancing!

He dances and sings.

Cocky-locky, necky neck.
Cockereekoo! Cockereekoo!
Henny-penny, pecky peck.
Cockereekoo! Cockereekoo!

ANITRA. You're sweating, master. Please don't melt. Let me carry that bag, dangling at your belt.

PEER. Yes, take it. How kind you are! I'm so happy today, it gets in the way.

He dances again.

ANITRA. It makes me happy to see Master dance.

PEER. Never mind 'master'. When we get to my castle –

ANITRA. Your Paradise. How far now?

PEER. A thousand miles.

ANITRA. Too far!

PEER. When we get there, you'll have the soul I promised.

ANITRA. I'll manage without. Goodbye!

She hits his hand free with the whip and gallops away, full tilt into the desert. PEER stands a long time as if thunderstruck.

PEER. Not again . . . !

24.

Same place. One hour later. PEER, *slowly and thoughtfully, is taking off his Muslim clothes, one by one. Finally he takes a small travelling-hat from his jacket pocket, puts it on, and stands there in his European clothes. He throws his turban away.*

PEER. There goes the Mahdi, and here stand I.
    That Sheikhish existence was no good at all.
    That minx! Just a hair's breadth from turning my head.
    You're a fool, Peer! Dancing to turn back the clock,
    To stem the tide. Prancing! Playing cocky-locky –
    Master! – No wonder you ended up plucked.
    Well, not quite. I've a little put by. Some here,
    Some in America. Not quite skint.
    I've enough – and who really needs more? Who needs
    Horses and coachmen and coffers and safes?
    I control my own destiny – who needs more?
    What next, then? There's plenty to choose from.
    An autobiography: fearless and frank . . .
    Inspirational . . . Or – I've got plenty of time –
    Archaeology . . . Got it! A wandering scholar!
    I'll travel and study the past.

Quietly moved:

    I'll sever the apron strings, once and for all.
    Cut all connection with family and friends.
    Riches? Forget 'em. Sweet nothings? No time.
    There's a mystery waiting, a riddle to solve –

He wipes away a tear.

    That's what engages a true man of science.
    Yes, master past history, inside and out.
    Step aside from the present. It's simply not worth it.
    The men are untrustworthy, spineless and clueless.

He shrugs his shoulders.

The women? Don't bother! The women are worse!

He goes.

25.

Summer day in the far north of Norway. PEER*'s hut in the forest. The door is open, its huge wooden bolt drawn back. Reindeer horns over the door. A flock of goats browsing beside the wall. A beautiful middle-aged woman,* SOLVEIG, *is sitting and spinning outside in the sunshine. She looks down the path and sings.*

SOLVEIG. Winter and spring may come and go;
    Summer too, the whole long year.
    But you'll come back one day, I know.
    I'll wait. I promised you, my dear.

    She calls to her goats, then spins and sings again.

    God guard you, dear, on land and sea,
    Or safe in heaven, before his throne.
    I'll wait till you come back to me,
    Or join you in heaven, my love, my own.

26.

Egypt. Dawn. The statue of Memnon stands in the sand. PEER *walks in and stands for a moment gazing round.*

PEER. Egypt. The statue of Memnon. Best place to start. No
    point going all the way back to the Creation.

    He sits on a rock.

I'll sit and wait till the statue sings its morning song. It never
fails. Then breakfast. Climb a pyramid. If time, look round
inside – then on to the Red Sea, to find King Potiphar's grave.

    He looks at his watch.

What a time sunrise takes! I'm not sure I can wait. Ah!
Something's happening. Tuning up.

    The sun rises. The STATUE *sings.*

STATUE. From the demigod's ashes fly
    Birds on high.
    Zeus made them, Zeus above,
    For war, not love.

Wise owl, declare:
My birds are sleeping where?
Solve the riddle. Try!
Speak up, or die!

PEER. Amazing. The voice of a statue. Music of the past. I'll
make a note. Ah well. On to Cairo, to see the Sphinx.

He writes in his notebook.

'Statue sang. Words clear; meaning obscure. Obviously a
hallucination from first to last. Apart from that, so far today,
nothing else of note.'

He goes out.

27.

*Near Gizeh village, next to the huge stone Sphinx. In the distance, the
spires and minarets of Cairo. PEER comes in. He examines the Sphinx
carefully, first through his pince-nez and then through the hollow of his
hand.*

PEER. The Sphinx. What an ugly brute! What on earth does it
remind me of? The Bøyg! That's it. The Bøyg I banged on the
brainpan. Or dreamed I did.

He goes closer.

Same eyes. Same lips. Bit wider-awake; craftier. Otherwise,
two peas in a pod. So you look like a lion in daylight, Bøyg?
Still fond of riddles? See if you answer like you did last time.

He calls out to the Sphinx.

Hey Bøyg, who are you?

VOICE (*from behind the Sphinx*). Ach, Sfinx, wer bist du?

PEER. An echo! I must note this down.

He writes in his book.

'German echo. Berlin accent.'

BEGRIFFENFELDT *comes out from behind the Sphinx.*

BEGRIFFENFELDT. A human!

PEER. Oh, it was hlm. (*Writing again.*) 'Later: same observation. Different conclusion.'

BEGRIFFENFELDT (*wildly excited*). Mein herr, excuse me. One vital question. Why did you come here *today*?

PEER. To see an old friend.

BEGRIFFENFELDT. The Sphinx?

PEER (*nodding*). I knew him years ago.

BEGRIFFENFELDT. You know him? Dear man! Then speak. Who is he?

PEER. Easy. He's himself.

BEGRIFFENFELDT (*jumping for joy*). Haha! In a flash, the riddle's solved. The riddle of the Sphinx! You say he's . . . himself?

PEER. So he told me.

BEGRIFFENFELDT. Himself. Enlightenment at last!

He takes off his hat.

Your name, dear man?

PEER. Peer Gynt.

BEGRIFFENFELDT (*entranced*). Peer Gynt! The Unknown, the Welcome Guest, whose coming was foretold.

PEER. You're joking. You came here to meet –

BEGRIFFENFELDT. Peer . . . Gynt! So deep! So strange! Each word a miracle of meaning. Who are you?

PEER (*modestly*). I've always tried to be . . . myself. Apart from that, my passport –

BEGRIFFENFELDT. So deep! So strange!

He takes PEER's hand.

To the city, come! To my . . . establishment. The . . . Institute I have the honour to direct. Enlightenment's emperor! Come!

He takes PEER's arm and drags him out.

28.

The Cairo madhouse. Large courtyard surrounded by high walls and buildings. Barred windows. Iron cages. Three keepers, MIKKEL, SCHLINGENBERG *and* SCHAFMANN, *are standing there. A fourth,* FUCHS, *comes in.*

FUCHS. Hey Schafmann, where's the Director?

SCHAFMANN. Went out, first thing.

FUCHS. Collecting.

MIKKEL. Shh! He's here!

BEGRIFFENFELDT *shows* PEER *in, locks the gate and pockets the key.*

PEER (*aside*). The man's a genius. I don't understand a word he says. (*Looking round.*) So this is your professors' club?

BEGRIFFENFELDT. Here they all are. The Seventy Savants, lock, stock and barrel. (*Shouting to the* WARDERS.) Mikkel, Schlingenberg, Schafmann, Fuchs, into the cages. Hop, hop, hop!

He locks the WARDERS *in cages, and throws the key down a well.*

PEER. Er . . . doctor . . . director . . .

BEGRIFFENFELDT. Don't call me that! I was once. Until . . . Master Gynt, can you keep a secret?

PEER (*increasingly uneasy*). What?

BEGRIFFENFELDT *takes him into a corner and whispers.*

BEGRIFFENFELDT. Last night, at eleven p.m., Common Sense . . . expired.

PEER. My God!

BEGRIFFENFELDT. A tragedy. Especially for me, in my position. Because up to then, up to that moment of catastrophe, this place was a madhouse.

PEER. Madhouse?

BEGRIFFENFELDT. Shh! Not any more! At eleven o'clock last night, all former lunatics became sane – and naturally, at precisely the same time, all so-called cleverdicks began to rave.

PEER. Time! That reminds me. I haven't much time . . .

BEGRIFFENFELDT. Of course.

He opens a door and shouts.

Come out! The promised time has come. Common sense is
dead. Long live Peer Gynt!

PEER. No no. It's quite all right . . .

The LUNATICS *come into the courtyard, one by one.*

BEGRIFFENFELDT. Good morning! Come and greet
freedom's dawn. Your emperor's here.

PEER. Too great an honour. I don't deserve –

BEGRIFFENFELDT. The man who solved the riddle of the
Sphinx? The man who is . . . himself?

PEER. Ah! That's the problem. I *am* myself. Completely. While
here, if I understand it right, you have to be beside yourself.

BEGRIFFENFELDT. Beside yourself? Not at all! People here are
one hundred per cent themselves. They sail as themselves,
full steam ahead. They climb into barrels of self, bung
themselves in with self, and pickle themselves in self. No one
weeps for others' suffering. No one cares what others think.
Utterly ourselves, in thought, word and deed. We need an
emperor – and you're our man.

PEER. Bloody hell.

BEGRIFFENFELDT. Don't be alarmed. You'll get used to it. 'Be
yourself' – look, I'll show you an example. The first that
comes along. (*To a dark passing figure.*) Morning, Huhu. How
are you? Still the picture of misery!

HUHU (*to* PEER). You're a stranger. Will you listen?

PEER (*bowing*). By all means.

HUHU. Lend me your ears.
In the east, like chains of daisies,
Lie the shores of Malabar.
Portuguese and Dutchmen landed,
Tried to civilise the natives.
In the forests (ancient forests)
Lived orangutangs. They'd been there
Since the dawn of hist'ry: screeching,

Brawling, lords and masters, free.
Then the foreign folk got busy,
Mixing up the ancient language,
Blurring prehistoric ways.
That's my mission. Clean the language,
Keep the forest tongue unsullied.
So, I screech. I march for screeching.
Folksongs in authentic screech.
Waste of time! Who notices? Who cares?
You lent your ears. Thanks. Now can you lend me some
advice?

PEER (*aside*). 'Go with the flow'. Isn't that what they say?
(*Aloud*):
Friend, if I remember rightly,
There are forests in Morocco
Bursting with orangutangs.
Pack your bags and go there. Join them.
If screech won't come to you, you go to screech.

HUHU. I'll do it! Thanks for listening. Off I go!

He goes, muttering and gesturing impressively.

BEGRIFFENFELDT. There! Wasn't he himself? Brimming over
with self. And here's another one. (*To an* EGYPTIAN *who is
walking past with a mummy on his back.*). How's it going, your
majesty?

EGYPTIAN (*to* PEER). I am king Apis, aren't I?

PEER (*getting behind* BEGRIFFENFELDT). I'm sorry, I don't
know his majesty personally. You certainly sound like him.

EGYPTIAN. You're lying. Just like the rest of them.

BEGRIFFENFELDT. Your majesty, please explain.

EGYPTIAN. Certainly. (*To* PEER.) You see this mummy I'm
carrying? King Apis. He's a mummy because he's dead. Built
the pyramids. Carved the mighty Sphinx. But the thing is, *I'm*
king Apis too. He was out hunting one day, and got off his
horse to piss in my grandfather's field. Next thing you know,
the corn grows, we harvest it and make our bread. That makes
me King Apis too. But d'you think anyone understands?
D'you think anyone bows down to me? King Apis! I don't
even *look* like him.

PEER. Your majesty, why don't you hang yourself? A few weeks in the coffin . . .

EGYPTIAN. Brilliant! My kingdom for a rope! I won't look much like him at first, but time'll see to that.

He goes to make arrangements to hang himself.

BEGRIFFENFELDT. A man with ambition.

PEER. Good God, he really is hanging himself! I feel sick! I'm dizzy.

BEGRIFFENFELDT. Transitional symptoms. They'll soon pass.

PEER. Transitional? What to? Excuse me, I've got to go.

BEGRIFFENFELDT. Are you crazy?

PEER. Not yet!

Uproar. HUSSEIN *comes in, pushing his way through the other* LUNATICS. *He goes to* PEER.

HUSSEIN. They say an emperor arrived today. That you?

PEER (*desperately*). They seem to think so.

HUSSEIN. In that case, sign these papers. And please, don't hesitate, dip me in. (*Bowing.*) I'm a quill. The trouble is, everyone takes me for a sandbox. They keep trying to shake sand out of me.

PEER. I was a silver-bound book once, in a woman's eyes.

HUSSEIN. The snag is, I'm blunt. What's the use of a blunt quill? I need sharpening. A knife, or the world ends here and now!

BEGRIFFENFELDT. Here's a knife.

HUSSEIN (*taking it*). Just watch me drink that ink!

He cuts his throat.

BEGRIFFENFELDT (*jumping clear*). You're splashing!.

PEER (*in growing alarm*). Hold him!

HUSSEIN. You heard him! Hold the pen! Put it to the paper.

He falls.

I'm done for. Write my postscript. 'He lived and died a pen, in other people's hands'.

PEER (*dizzy*). How can I . . . ? What am I . . .? God above, I'll be
    anything you like . . . troll, mahdi, sinner. Just help me!
    Protector of madmen, help!

He faints and falls. BEGRIFFENFELDT, *with a crown of straw in
his hand, jumps and sits astride him.*

BEGRIFFENFELDT. Enthroned in mud. Beside himself at last.

He crowns PEER.

Long live the emperor of self!

LUNATICS. Long live the emperor of self!

29.

*On board a ship in the North Sea, off the Norwegian coast. Sunset.
Storm brewing.* PEER, *a vigorous old man with ice-grey hair and beard,
stands on the poop deck, aft. He leans on the rail and gazes towards
land. He is dressed partly as a sailor, in pea-jacket and seaboots. His
clothes are shabby and worn, and he himself looks weatherbeaten and
leathery. The* CAPTAIN *and* HELMSMAN *are at the wheel; the*
CREW *are forard.*

PEER. After all these years, to be sailing home. To see the
    mountains of Norway. There's Hallingskarven, dressed for
    winter. That's Jøkel behind him. Behind them both,
    Folgefånn, like a girl in shining white. Don't get ideas, any of
    you! You're just lumps of granite. Stay where you are!

CAPTAIN (*shouting forard*). Two men to the wheel! Hoist the
    light!

PEER. It's blowing.

CAPTAIN. We'll have a storm tonight.

PEER. Can you see Ronde from the sea?

CAPTAIN. Hardly. Fonnen's in the way.

PEER. Ah yes.

CAPTAIN. You know this coast?

PEER. I passed this way when I left the country. Last seen,
    longest remembered, as they say.

He spits and gazes out at the coast.

There, where the fells are blue, in the dark, narrow valleys, down to the wide fjords: that's where people live.

He looks at the CAPTAIN.

Not many houses here.

CAPTAIN. Few and far between.

PEER. Shall we be in by dawn?

CAPTAIN. If the night goes easy.

PEER. It's gathering out west.

CAPTAIN. It is.

PEER. By the way, remind me when we settle up. I'd like to give the crew a little something. You know what I mean.

CAPTAIN. Thanks. They're none of them wealthy men. They've all got wives and children. Their pay spreads thin. A little extra from you will make this a homecoming to remember.

PEER. Did you say wives and children?

CAPTAIN. Every man jack of them. Cook's the poorest of the lot. In his house, they've never enough to eat.

PEER. Married? Someone waiting? Glad to see them home?

CAPTAIN. That's right. Poor people live like that.

PEER. Suppose they arrive late? In the evening?

CAPTAIN. I imagine their wives will have something tasty waiting. A special treat.

PEER. A candle on the table?

CAPTAIN. Two, maybe. A drop to drink –

PEER. They'll sit there, warm and snug? Children round them? Chatter and noise? Pure happiness?

CAPTAIN. Very likely. And this time, all thanks to you. Your little present.

PEER (*punching the gunwale*). Oh no! D'you take me for an idiot? Forking out for other people's children! I worked hard to make my pile. No one's waiting for old Peer Gynt.

CAPTAIN. It's your money. Anything you say. Excuse me. The wind's rising.

He walks away across the deck. Darkness has fallen, and lights are being lit in the cabin. The sea grows rougher. Mist and cloud gather.

PEER. A houseful of children, waiting to welcome you. Good wishes to speed you on your way. And no one cares a straw for me. Candles on the table? I'll snuff 'em! I'll spoil their fun!

The ship rolls heavily. He staggers and holds on with difficulty.

That was a bad one. The sea's working overtime tonight.

He listens.

Someone shouting.

WATCH (*forard*). Wreck to leeward!

CAPTAIN (*amidships, shouting orders*). Hard a starboard! Hug the wind!

HELMSMAN. Are there any survivors?

WATCH. Three. I think.

PEER. Lower a boat.

CAPTAIN. It'd be swamped.

He goes forard.

PEER. Never mind. (*To some of the* CREW.) Fellow human beings! Help them! What're you scared of – a ducking?

BOATSWAIN. No hope in sea like this.

PEER. More shouts. The wind's howling. Cook, you try. Go on! I'll pay you.

COOK. Not for twenty pounds.

PEER. Bastards! Cowards! They've wives and children waiting.

CAPTAIN. Run on!

HELMSMAN. The wreck's gone down.

The storm grows worse. PEER *goes astern.*

PEER. In weather like tonight's, look out for God. *I'm* all right. I offered money: I'm not to blame. My trouble is, I'm too easygoing. I always get the blame. If I were younger, I'd play things differently. Show them who was boss. There's still time.

Let word get round that Peer Gynt's home in triumph! Some
way or other, I'll get back the farm, rebuild it . . . gleaming as
a castle. Then – visitors, keep out! Stand in the doorway, cap
in hand. Shuffle your feet. Beg how you like, you won't get a
penny! I've had to suffer the lashing of destiny – now just
watch me! I'll give twice as good as I got.

A STRANGER, *standing in the gloom beside* PEER, *greets him
cheerily.*

STRANGER. Good evening.

PEER. Who on Earth are you?

STRANGER. Fellow passenger. Pleased to meet you.

PEER. Fellow passenger? I'm the only one.

STRANGER. I don't go out in daylight.

PEER. Aren't you well? You're white as a sheet.

STRANGER. Fine, thank you.

PEER. What a storm.

STRANGER. Wonderful, isn't it? Waves like houses.
    Mouthwatering. Think of all the wrecks tonight . . . the
    corpses washed up on shore.

PEER. God forbid!

STRANGER. Have you ever seen a corpse? Hanged, say?
    Drowned?

PEER. What d'you mean?

STRANGER. They grin. Forced laughter. Most bite their
    tongues.

PEER. Get out of here!

STRANGER. Just one question. Suppose . . . just suppose . . . we
    run aground in the darkness . . . Suppose I end up saved, and
    you end up drowned –

PEER (*feeling in his pocket*). What are you after? Money?

STRANGER. No. But if you'd be good enough . . . your
    Excellency's corpse.

PEER. You're crazy!

STRANGER. Just your corpse. Donated to science –

PEER. Get stuffed!

STRANGER. Bad moment? I understand. Later on, then.

He bows in a friendly way.

I'll talk to you when you're sinking. You'll be in a better temper then.

He goes into the cabin.

PEER. Scientists! Brrr! Atheists . . . (*To the* BOATSWAIN, *who is passing.*) Just a minute. Who was that passenger? That lunatic?

BOATSWAIN. You're the only one.

PEER. It gets worse and worse. (*To a* CREWMAN, *who is coming out of the cabin.*) Who went into the cabin just now?

CREWMAN. The ship's dog, sir.

He goes.

WATCH (*calling out*). Land ahoy!

PEER. My box! My chest! Bring them up on deck.

BOATSWAIN. We're busy.

PEER. I was joking, Captain! Playing the fool. Of course I'll help the cook.

CAPTAIN. The jib's gone.

HELMSMAN. And the foresail.

BOATSWAIN (*shouting forard*). Rocks ahead!

CAPTAIN. Smashed to smithereens!

Panic and confusion, as the ship strikes the rocks.

30.

Offshore. Rocks and waves. The ship is sinking. In the mist, a boat with two men in it. A wave fills it and it overturns. Screams, then silence. After a moment the boat's hull comes into sight, with PEER *beside it.*

PEER. Help! Send a lifeboat! Help! I'm drowning!

He clings to the upturned boat. The COOK *surfaces on the other side.*

COOK. Oh God! Mercy! For my children's sake! Help me up!

He grabs the hull.

PEER. Cook! Let go.

COOK. You let go.

PEER. It won't take two.

COOK. I know. Get off.

PEER. You get off.

They struggle. The COOK's *free hand is hurt, but he clings on with the other one.*

Let go!

COOK. Have mercy! Think of my kids at home.

PEER. I've still to have my kids.

COOK. You've had your life. I've hardly started.

PEER. Sink! Get on with it! You're fat enough.

COOK. Be generous. Let go. Who'll miss you?

He shrieks and slips.

I'm drowning!

PEER *grabs him.*

PEER. I've got your hair. Say a prayer. 'Our father'.

COOK. I've forgotten it.

PEER. Say any of it. Hurry up!

COOK. 'Give us this day . . .'

PEER. It's easy to guess your profession.

His grip loosens. The COOK *sinks.*

COOK. 'Give us this day' -

He goes under.

PEER. Amen. He was himself, right to the end.

He climbs on the upturned hull.

Where there's life, there's hope.

The STRANGER *takes hold of the boat.*

STRANGER. Good evening.

PEER. You again! Let go! There's no room.

STRANGER. I'll wedge my finger in this crack. I'll be all right.
It's about your corpse.

PEER. Shut up.

STRANGER. Whatever you say.

Pause.

PEER. Well?

STRANGER. I've shut up.

PEER. Bloody hell! What do you want?

STRANGER. I'm waiting.

PEER (*tearing his hair*). I'll go mad! Who are you?

STRANGER. A friend.

PEER (*after a pause*). Well?

STRANGER. Don't you recognise me?

PEER. The Devil –

STRANGER (*whispering*). Shh! Does he light our way when all
seems dark?

PEER. Ah yes. An angel of mercy, are you?

STRANGER. Friend, have you ever – say, twice a year – been
really scared out of your wits?

PEER. Everyone's scared when danger comes.

STRANGER. And have you ever – say, once in your life – felt the
exhilaration terror brings?

PEER (*giving him a look*). If you've come to reform me, you're an
idiot to leave it so late. Why should I change when I'm just
about to drown?

STRANGER. You'd feel more triumph in your armchair, sitting
beside your fire?

PEER. Leave me alone. Bugger off. I won't die. I'll get to land.

STRANGER. Of course you will. No one ever dies in the middle
of Act Five.

He disappears.

PEER. I might have guessed. A critic!

31.

Churchyard, high in the hills. Funeral. PRIEST *and* MOURNERS.
The last verse of a hymn is being sung. PEER *is passing, and stops at
the gate.*

PEER. A churchyard. High up here in the hills! Some poor devil
going the way of all flesh. Thank God it isn't me!

He goes in. The PRIEST *is speaking over the grave.*

PRIEST. Dear friends, his soul stands at the judgement seat.
    A word about his time down here on Earth.
    I'll not forget one morning, years ago,
    When soldiers came recruiting here at Lunde.
    Wartime. Our country's need in all men's minds.
    Behind the table sat an officer,
    Some sergeants and the mayor. Our young men came
    Before them one by one, and one by one
    They were examined, enlisted and sent to war.
    A name was called. A lad came in. His face
    Was white as a snowfield. His right hand wrapped
    In a cloth. He swallowed, swayed and gasped for breath.
    At last, fiery-faced, he stammered out his tale:
    A sickle had slipped and sliced his finger off.
    Silence. Pursed lips. They stoned him with their looks.
    The officer stood up – an old, grey man -
    Spat, pointed his finger and said just one word: 'Out!'
    The boy stumbled to the door, took to his heels
    And ran: up the fellside, through woods and fields,
    Slipping and sliding, to the high, bleak moors.

    Six months passed. Back he came, with mother, wife
    And child. Leased land on the fellside, built a house,
    Began to plough. He made his way, as corn

In yellow patches proved among the stones.
In church he kept his right hand in his pocket;
On the farm nine fingers worked as well as ten.
Three sons he had, three sturdy lads. They went
To school, a long way off. No road. He let
The eldest climb and scramble as best he could,
Roped for safety, and carried the other two
Himself. Year followed year. They're grown up now.
In America they prosper. None thinks now
Of his father in Norway, who carried him to school.

A humble man. Humble. Branded with shame
From the time his cheeks flamed red on Enlistment day.
Hand hidden in his pocket. Out of sight.
A traitor? No patriot? Perhaps. Up there,
In his own small circle, where his work lay, there
He was a hero. There he was himself,
His metal rang true. His life was one long tune
Played on muted strings. He fought his own small war,
The peasant's war, and fell. May he rest in peace!

The MOURNERS *separate and leave.* PEER *alone remains.*

PEER. Now that's what I call Christianity! That's what I call
religion! Pah! Who needs it? Just be yourself. It's time I went
home.

He goes.

32.

*Hillside with dried up stream and ruined mill. The ground is derelict
and strewn with rubbish. Higher up, a big farmhouse: Haegstad, where
the wedding was in Part I. Outside the farmhouse, an auction. Crowd;
drink; noise.* PEER *is sitting on a rubbish tip beside the mill.*

PEER. In or out, it's just as far. This side or that, it's just as
narrow. Time gnaws; the stream divides. 'Go round', said the
Bøyg, and so I must.

MAN IN MOURNING (ASLAK *from Part 1*). Some auction!
There's nothing left but junk.

He sees PEER.

A stranger! Afternoon, old man.

PEER. And to you. Why the party? A christening? A wedding?

MAN IN MOURNING. Not a chance. Property auction. The
owner's pushing up daisies.

PEER. That'll please the worms.

MAN IN MOURNING. Everything ends. I was a blacksmith
once. End of story.

PEER. All stories end the same way. When I was a lad, I knew
them all.

YOUNG MAN (*with a casting-ladle*). Look what I bought! Peer
Gynt's old casting-ladle.

PEER. Peer Gynt? Who was he?

MAN IN MOURNING. Family. Just family. Hers – the dead one.
And Aslak's – her husband.

MAN IN GREY (MADS MOEN *from Part 1*). Don't forget Mads
Moen! His too.

MAN IN MOURNING. You and that hayloft. Ha!

MAN IN GREY. What's it matter? We're all family. All of us here
at Haegstad. Peer Gynt's close kin.

He and MAN IN MOURNING *go off together.*

PEER (*aside*). Old acquaintance! (*Aloud.*) Bring brandy, lads!
I'm feeling my age. I'll auction all my junk.

YOUNG MAN. What have you got to sell?

PEER. A castle. High on the hill.

YOUNG MAN. I bid one button.

PEER. Make it a drink. It's an insult to offer less.

A crowd gathers round. PEER *calls the lots.*

PEER. Grane, my horse.

SOMEONE IN THE CROWD. Where?

PEER. Beyond the sunset. He flies as fast as . . . as Peer Gynt's
lies.

VOICES. What else? What else?

PEER. My empire. Fight for it!

YOUNG MAN. Is there a crown?

PEER. Of finest straw. Fits whoever puts it on. Here's more! A rotten egg. A madman's hair. A Mahdi's beard. Take them all – just show me the hillside where the signpost says, 'This way!'

The STEWARD *comes in.*

STEWARD. That's enough now. Any more, and you're in trouble.

PEER (*hat in hand*). Thank you kindly. Just a minute. Who was Peer Gynt?

STEWARD. Who cares?

PEER. I mean it.

STEWARD. A hopeless case. A yarnspinner.

PEER. Yarnspinner?

STEWARD. Great deeds. Heroic adventures. Made out he'd done them all. Now, excuse me. I've things to do.

He goes.

PEER. And where is he now, this remarkable man?

ELDERLY MAN. Sailed away. Foreign parts. Came to a bad end. Hanged, years ago.

PEER. I might have guessed. Himself to the end: the late Peer Gynt. (*Bowing.*) Time to be going. I've really enjoyed myself.

He goes a short way, then turns back.

Ladies and gentlemen, shall I pay you with a story?

SEVERAL. Yes. If you know one.

PEER. Oh yes. Yes indeed.

He goes closer. His expression has completely changed.

> I was in San Francisco, digging for gold.
> The whole town swarmed with freaks.
> 'I play the fiddle with my toes.'
> 'I dance fandangos on my knees.'
> 'I make up poems while my assistant here
> Bores portholes in my skull.'

Next thing we knew, the Devil himself
Turned up. Auditioning, of course.
His act was grunting like a pig.
In he swept, in his flowing cloak –
With a porker underneath, though no one knew.
The act began. The Devil pinched. The piggy squealed.
An entire pig lifecycle, wild *and* tame,
Ending with the squeal on the butcher's block.
One last deep bow, and off he went –
Leaving the rest of us divided.
'Wonderfully lifelike!' 'Overdone!'
'Too muffled!' 'That dying squeal –
Pure melodrama!' Each one, a different detail –
But all agreed in one particular:
No real pig ever uttered quite like that.
Poor old Devil. Forgot the first rule
Of showbusiness: don't outsmart your audience.

He bows and goes, leaving a baffled silence.

33.

Whitsun Eve. Clearing, deep in the forest. In the background, a hut with reindeer horns over the doorway. PEER *is crawling about in the undergrowth, digging up wild onions.*

PEER. Another chapter over. What comes next? Try everything once. Self-sufficiency. Fill your belly: rule number one. H'm. Wild onions . . . Later on I'll get organised: set some traps. There's water in the beck: I won't die of thirst. And when I die – no avoiding it! – I'll crawl under a fallen tree like a bear, cover myself with leaves and write on the trunk: 'Here lies Peer Gynt. Not a bad chap. The Forest Kaiser.' Kaiser! (*Laughing to himself.*) Credulous old fool! You're an onion, not an emperor. I'll peel you, Peer.

He takes an onion and peels it, layer by layer.

That's the tattered outer layer. Shipwrecked man, clinging to his boat. Next the passenger, skinny and lanky – still tastes a bit of Gynt. Gold-digger next. No nourishment there. Someone's snaffled that. Tough skin next, with hard edges: fur-trapper in Hudson's Bay. Ha! A crown. No thanks: throw that away, no comment. Archaeologist, small but wiry. Mahdi. Ha, very fresh: stinks of lies. My eyes are watering.

He plucks off several layers at once.

What a lot of layers! Do we never reach the heart?

He pulls the whole thing to pieces.

Christ, never! There's nothing else but layers. Smaller and smaller. Nature's little joke!

He throws the pieces down, and scratches his head.

Bloody marvellous! Life – if you call it life – holds all the aces, and if *you* win a hand, hop! skip! He's off. You've nothing.

He has come near the hut. He gives a start.

A hut! In the middle of nowhere. (*Rubbing his eyes.*) Looks very familiar. Reindeer horns over the door. A mermaid, fish from the navel down. Rubbish! There's no mermaid . . . just nails and planks, and a bolt against goblin-thoughts!

SOLVEIG (*singing inside the hut*).The feast is set, my dear.
    Where'er you roam,
    Will you come home
    This year?
    Say, is your burden great?
    Be easy, Peer.
    I'll always wait,
    I swear.

    PEER *stands still and white.*

PEER. One who remembered and one who forgot.
    One who was faithful and one who betrayed.
    O heavy beyond all lightening!
    Heart's grief! It was here my empire lay.

He hurries away, down the path into the forest.

34.

Night. Moor, once covered with firs, now made desert by a forest fire. Charred tree stumps for miles in all directions. Wisps of white mist here and there, low over the ground. PEER hurries in.

PEER. Ashes, mist and wind-blown dust-clouds –
     Just the stuff I need to work with.
     Stench and foulness deep inside me –
     What a whited sepulchre!
     Daydreams, tales and stillborn fancies
     Make the base I need to build.
     See the pyramid climb skywards
     With its scaffolding of lies.
     On the summit fly this banner:
     'No more honesty. No regrets!'
     Let the trumpets sound my motto:
     'Peer did this. Peer Kaiser Gynt!'

   He listens.

     Voices! Children's voices, crying,
     Singing. Threadballs underfoot!
     Trolls, up here on empty moorland.

   He kicks at them.

     Clear off out! You're in my way!

THREADBALLS (*on the ground*). We are thoughts.
     You should have thought us.
     Given us tootsies,
     Let us run.

PEER (*stumbling over them*). Threadballs! Cheeky devils!
     Watch it! Leave my feet alone.

   He hurries from them.

WITHERED LEAVES (*blowing on the wind*). We are words.
     You should have said us.
     Passwords, wasted,
     Never used.

PEER. Withered leaves! Who needs you?
     Lie there on the ground and rot.

WHISTLING IN THE WIND. We are songs.
     You should have sung us.
     Poison choke you!
     Voice-box rot!

PEER. Whistling in the wind! You choke!
     Boring! Gibberish! Get stuffed.

DEWDROPS (*falling from the trees*). We are tears.
  You should have wept us.
  Ice-blades turning
  In the heart.

PEER. Thanks. I wept at Ronde,
  And someone kicked me up the bum.

BROKEN STRAWS. We are deeds.
  You should have done us.
  Wait till judgement.
  Then we'll tell.

PEER. Bastards! Sneaks! Make trouble
  Telling what I *didn't* do?

ÅSE'S VOICE (*far off*). Watch where you're driving!
  Look where you've dumped me,
  Here in this snowdrift.
  I'm soaking. I'm aching.
  Can't you be careful?
  Where is that castle?
  The Devil took over
  As soon as you picked up that whip!

PEER. Off I go. No point in staying.
  Bad enough to bear one's own sins.
  Bear the Devil's too, you're done for:
  Might as well be six feet under.

  He hurries out.

35.

Another part of the moor. The BUTTON MOULDER, *with his box of tools and a large casting ladle, comes in along a side path.*

BUTTON MOULDER. Hello, old man.

PEER. Good evening, friend.

BUTTON MOULDER. In a hurry? What are you doing, here on this empty moor?

PEER. Moving towards my death. What else?

BUTTON MOULDER. Ah. Excuse me . . . my eyes aren't what they were. Are you Peer Gynt?

PEER. So people say.

BUTTON MOULDER. Perfect! The man I was sent to find.

PEER. What for?

BUTTON MOULDER. Easy. I'm a button moulder. You're to go in my ladle.

PEER. Why?

BUTTON MOULDER. To be melted down.

PEER. Pardon?

BUTTON MOULDER. Here's the ladle, wiped and waiting. Your grave's dug. Your coffin's ordered. Your body will feast the worms. My orders are to fetch your soul to the Boss at once.

PEER. Without a word of notice?

BUTTON MOULDER. That's how it's always done. Births . . . burials. Day chosen on the quiet. Not a word to the guest of honour.

PEER. I don't feel well. Oh Peer! What an end to your journey! I wasn't all that bad. An idiot, perhaps. Not a proper sinner.

BUTTON MOULDER. Precisely. Not a proper sinner. That's why you escape the pincers, and go to the casting ladle with the others.

PEER. You're going to melt me down with every Tom, Dick and Harry, and start again?

BUTTON MOULDER. That's right. Like worn out coins.

PEER. I refuse. I won't.

BUTTON MOULDER. What's all the fuss about? It's not important. You were never yourself, alive – why do you care what happens when you're dead?

PEER. Never myself? You're joking! Never myself – Peer Gynt? What else have I ever been? I'm Peer. All Peer.

BUTTON MOULDER. Can't be. I've got my orders. Look:

'Fetch Gynt. He's totally missed his way. Faulty merchandise –
straight into the ladle.'

PEER. It's nonsense! You've got the wrong Gynt. Are you sure it
means Peer? Not Rasmus . . . Jon?

BUTTON MOULDER. I melted them down years ago.

PEER. Give me time.

BUTTON MOULDER. What for?

PEER. To prove I've been myself.

BUTTON MOULDER. How will you prove it?

PEER. Witnesses. Sworn statements.

BUTTON MOULDER. The Boss won't like those.

PEER. Of course he will. Just lend me myself, for a little while. I
won't run away. It's only natural, once you've got a self, to
fight to keep it. Please!

BUTTON MOULDER. All right. But remember: at the next
crossroads, we meet again.

PEER goes.

36.

Deeper in the moor. PEER *hurries in.*

PEER. Time's money, or so they say. If I only knew how far the
crossroads were. A witness! Where will I find a witness, here in
this forest? There's something wrong with the world, if you
have to have proof of rights which are as clear as day.

A bent OLD MAN *(the* OLD MAN OF THE MOUNTAIN *from
Part I) hobbles up to him. He leans on a stick and carries a bag on his
back.*

OLD MAN. Spare a penny for a poor old man.

PEER. Sorry. No change.

OLD MAN. Prince Peer! It can't be. After all these years.

PEER. Who are you?

OLD MAN. The Old Man. Have you forgotten?

PEER. The troll king? You?

OLD MAN. I've had dreadful luck.

PEER. Witnesses like this don't grow on trees.

OLD MAN. Your highness has gone a little grey since last we met.

PEER. Old age, father in law, gnawing and tearing. Don't let's rake up the past. Especially our little disagreement. It was all my fault.

OLD MAN. No no. Your highness was young. It happens to us all. In any case, your highness was lucky to lose that bride. She was nothing but trouble. As soon as you left, she went from bad to worse.

PEER. Impossible!

OLD MAN. *And* my grandson sprouted. Big . . . broad. Bouncing babies, sown in every field.

PEER. Look . . . father in law . . . not just now. I've a lot on my mind. I need a reference. You're just the person. Let's have a drink, for old time's sake. I think I can find the cash.

OLD MAN. Your highness! Can I really be of service? Perhaps you could give *me* a reference.

PEER. Not now. Listen. You remember that night I came courting your daughter?

OLD MAN. Of course, your highness.

PEER. Never mind the highness. You wanted to operate . . . carve my eyeball . . . make Peer Gynt a troll. What did I do? Flat refusal. Said I'd stand on my own two feet. Gave up marriage, power, honour – to be myself. All I want you to do is swear to that.

OLD MAN. I can't.

PEER. Pardon?

OLD MAN. I can't swear lies. Everything you say . . . it was just the opposite.

PEER. You what?

OLD MAN. When you left the mountain, you took our motto.
Printed in your brain.

PEER. What motto?

OLD MAN. The one that sorts out trolls from human beings.
'Be true to yourself – ish'.

PEER (*recoiling*). Selfish!

OLD MAN. And ever since, you've lived your life by it.

PEER. Me? Peer Gynt?

OLD MAN (*weeping*). It's so ungrateful. To live like a troll, and
keep it dark. The word I taught you gave you the chance to
live like a man of means. Now you come here, and what
thanks do I get? You throw it in my face.

PEER. Me – a troll?

OLD MAN. No doubt about it.

PEER. You mean I could have stayed here in Norway all the
time? In peace and quiet? Saved all that effort, all that
heartache, all those pairs of shoes? Peer Gynt – a troll! Shut
up! You're mad. You're senile. Find an old Trolls' home.

OLD MAN. I wish I could. But my grandson keeps telling
people I don't exist. I'm a folk tale. Family! They're the worst.
It's very hard to be a legend.

PEER. I know what you mean.

OLD MAN. It's not as if we had troll charities . . . banks . . .
savings accounts. They weren't our style.

PEER. Didn't suit that bloody 'Be true to yourselfish'.

OLD MAN. Your highness. You did all right. Can't you see your
way . . . ?

PEER. Not a penny. It's not just you that's down and out. And
it's all your fault. Fucking trolls! I knew I should have kept
away!

OLD MAN. Ah well. I'm off. I'm going to town.

PEER. What for?

OLD MAN. National Theatre. Character work.

PEER. Break a leg. If my luck doesn't improve, I'll join you.

He hurries off down the path, leaving the OLD MAN *calling after him.*

37.

Crossroads.

PEER. You're in big trouble, Peer. Big trouble. That 'selfish' was a bad mistake. Your ship's going down. Cling to the wreckage. Anything to avoid the scrap heap.

BUTTON MOULDER (*at the crossroads*). Hi, Peer. Got your witnesses?

PEER. Crossroads already? That was quick.

BUTTON MOULDER. I can read you like a signpost. I know what's in your mind.

PEER. I'm tired of running. Not knowing the way.

BUTTON MOULDER. Getting nowhere fast.

PEER. It's the forest . . . the darkness . . .

BUTTON MOULDER. There's a tramp back there. Shall we call him?

PEER. Leave him. He's a drunk.

BUTTON MOULDER. But couldn't he – ?

PEER. Leave him, I said.

BUTTON MOULDER. Let's get on with it, then.

PEER. One question. What's it mean, to be yourself?

BUTTON MOULDER. Funny question, from someone who's just –

PEER. Just the same, please answer.

BUTTON MOULDER. To be yourself is to destroy your Self. D'you get it? No?

PEER. Listen: I give up my claim to be myself. It's too hard to prove. In any case, when I was wandering about the moor just now, my conscience really began giving me hell. I said to myself, 'You're a sinner . . .'

BUTTON MOULDER. Not that again.

PEER. No no. A real sinner. Not just deeds, but thoughts and words. I lived a shocking life abroad.

BUTTON MOULDER. But can you prove it?

PEER. Give me time. I'll find a priest, make my confession and bring you the documents.

BUTTON MOULDER. But –

PEER. Go on! It's not as if you're run off your feet up here. Hardly anyone ever dies.

BUTTON MOULDER. The next crossroads. No further.

PEER. A priest. Somewhere there has to be a priest.

He hurries out.

38.

Heathery slope. Path winding up the hill.

PEER. Waste not, want not, as the man said when he picked up the magpie's wing. Who'd have thought sins would turn out so useful in the end?

A THIN PERSON *hurries down the hill. He is wearing a cassock with its skirts looped up, and carrying a large bird-net.*

Hey up. It's my lucky day. Evening, father. Uphill work!

THIN PERSON. But worth it to win a soul.

PEER. Someone going to heaven?

THIN PERSON. Another place entirely.

PEER. Father, d'you mind if I –

THIN PERSON. Not at all. Nice to have company.

PEER. You see, I've always kept strictly to the law. Never been in trouble. Even so, a man trips up now and then, stumbles . . .

THIN PERSON. Happens to the best of us.

PEER. You understand, these trifles –

THIN PERSON. Trifles?

PEER. I never went in for sins in bulk.

THIN PERSON. In that case: sorry. You're wasting my time. I'm not who you think I am. See these fingers?

PEER. Long nails. Very long.

THIN PERSON. And these feet?

PEER (*pointing*). Is that hoof real?

THIN PERSON. My pride and joy.

PEER (*raising his hat*). It's an honour to meet you. I'd have sworn you were a priest. But this is much better. If the front door's open, don't use the back. If you can talk to his lordship, stuff the butler.

THIN PERSON. A man without prejudice! Shake hands. My dear fellow, how can I help you? Just don't ask for power or cash.

PEER. Ah. Well. What I'd really like . . .

THIN PERSON. A corner of your own.

PEER. You took the words out of my mouth. Nothing lavish. You'd hardly ever notice.

THIN PERSON. Somewhere warm?

PEER. Not too warm. The main thing is, to be able to come and go as I like. Go, especially.

THIN PERSON. My dear chap, I'm sorry. You've no idea how often I get the same request.

PEER. But when I think back over my life . . . I'm the ideal customer.

THIN PERSON. Trifles, you said.

PEER. In a way. I did take idols into China.

THIN PERSON. Peanuts.

PEER. I passed myself off as a Mahdi.

THIN PERSON. Small potatoes. I have my standards.

PEER. All right. I was shipwrecked. Perched on an upturned boat. The ship's cook drowned. It was half my fault.

THIN PERSON. Half a sin! We don't waste fuel on semi-sinners. Now if you'll excuse me, I've got to go. I've a steak to grill. Really juicy. No time to stand here gossiping.

PEER. May I ask what his sin was – this . . . steak . . .?

THIN PERSON. As I understand it, day and night, he never stopped being himself.

PEER. Himself? You punish people for being themselves?

THIN PERSON. Depends. We leave the door ajar. You can be yourself two ways. Like a jacket, inside out or outside in. D'you know, someone in Paris has just invented a way to take pictures using sunlight. Some look like the original, but others are what they call 'negatives', reversing light and shade. They look rubbish if you just glance at them, but they contain a likeness just the same. You have to bring it out. It's exactly the same with souls. If someone's soul-photograph is negative, it's not chucked out. They send the plate to me for processing. I steam it, dip it, burn it, rinse it, with sulphur and . . . so on, till the proper likeness comes. Negative turns positive.

PEER. Ah. H'm. May I ask whose name is on the negative you're working on?

THIN PERSON. Peter Gynt.

PEER. Peter Gynt? Aha! And Mr Gynt's himself?

THIN PERSON. So he says.

PEER. He's right then. Never mind negative and positive. He never lies.

THIN PERSON. You know him?

PEER. Nodding acquaintance.

THIN PERSON. I'm in a hurry. Where did you see him last?

PEER. Down at the Cape.

THIN PERSON. Good Hope?

PEER. He was just about to leave.

THIN PERSON. I'll have to run. I hope I'm in time. I hate the Cape. Too full of missionaries from Stavanger.

He hurries out.

PEER. Pillock! Look at him! He's just not up to it. He'll be out
on his neck if he doesn't look out. H'm. I'm not so secure
myself. Chucked out from the self-owning classes.

A shooting star shines overhead. He nods to it.

Peer Gynt salutes you, brother star. Shine . . . fade . . . vanish
in empty space . . .

Nervously, he pulls himself together and goes further into the mist.
Pause, and then he shouts:

Is there no one? No one in all creation? In heaven? In hell?

He returns, throws his hat on the ground and tears his hair. He
gradually grows calmer.

Beautiful Earth, forgive me
For pointlessly treading you.
Beautiful Sun, you wasted
Your rays on an empty house.
Life! What a price to pay
For being born. Now let me go up:
To the peaks, to the highest tips
To see the sunrise, to tire my eyes
Gazing out at the promised land.
Then let a snowdrift cover me;
Let them write 'No one. R.I.P.' –
And after that, who gives a damn?

WORSHIPPERS (*singing on the road*).
Come, Holy Ghost, our souls inspire,
And lighten with celestial fire;
Thou the anointing spirit art,
Who dost thy sevenfold gifts impart.

PEER (*cringing with terror*). Don't look! It's a mirage! Don't let
me be dead before I die!

He tries to hide in the bushes, but finds himself at the crossroads.

BUTTON MOULDER. Well, Peer? Your list of sins?

PEER. I've shouted and whistled. I've done my best.

BUTTON MOULDER. No one came?

PEER. Just a travelling photographer.

BUTTON MOULDER. O.K. Time's up.

PEER (*pointing*). What's that, shining?

BUTTON MOULDER. Nothing. Light in a house.

PEER. What's that noise?

BUTTON MOULDER. A woman, singing.

PEER. That's it! That's where I'll hear my sins.

They have left the trees and are standing by a hut. Dawn.

BUTTON MOULDER. One more crossroads, Peer. The last.

He steps aside and goes. PEER *goes towards the hut.*

PEER. In or out, it's just as far. This side or that, it's just as narrow.

He stops.

The voice is calling me: come in, come back, come home.

He takes a few steps, then stops again.

Go round, said the Bøyg.

He hears singing from the hut.

Not this time! Straight ahead, however hard!

He hurries towards the hut. At the same moment
SOLVEIG *comes to the door, dressed for church and carrying a prayerbook wrapped in a handkerchief. She is all but blind, and guides her steps with a stick. She stands there, upright and gentle.* PEER *hurls himself down on the threshold.*

Forgive me! Oh forgive my sins!

SOLVEIG. It's him. Praise God! It's him!

She gropes to find him.

PEER. Tell me my sins, how deep my guilt.

SOLVEIG. No guilt. No sins. My love!

She gropes for him again, and finds him.

BUTTON MOULDER (*from behind the hut*). Peer Gynt, the list!

PEER. Cry out my sins!

SOLVEIG (*sitting beside him*). You've made my life a beautiful song. God bless you for coming, for coming at Whitsuntide.

PEER. I'm done for. Unless you guess the riddle.

SOLVEIG. What riddle?

PEER. What riddle? Ha! Where has Peer Gynt been?

SOLVEIG. Been?

PEER. Yes! With his destiny on his brow. Since he sprang from the mind of God. Can you answer? If you can't, I must go home – down to the shadow land.

SOLVEIG (*smiling*). The answer's easy.

PEER. You know? Where I've been? Myself, entire, complete – Peer Gynt, with God's stamp on my brow?

SOLVEIG. In my faith. In my hope. In my love.

PEER (*starting back*). What? Your love? In your love? My . . . self exists in that?

He seems suddenly transfigured. He cries:

PEER. Hide me, then, oh hide me in your love!

He clings to her and buries his face in her lap. Long pause. The sun rises.

SOLVEIG (*singing softly*).
Sleep my sweetheart, sleep my child,
I will guard you, meek and mild.
Baby sits on mother's knee,
Playing together, he and she.
Baby lies in mother's arms,
Safe and sound from all that harms.
Baby sleeps in blissful rest,
Safe and sound on mother's breast.
Sleep my sweetheart, sleep my child,
I will guard you, meek and mild.

BUTTON MOULDER (*from behind the hut*). The last crossroads, Peer Gynt! I say no more.

SOLVEIG (*singing louder in the sun*).
I will guard you, meek and mild,
Sleep and dream my darling child.

The End